SUPER EASY SONGBOOK

DISNEY

W9-CSU-734

The following songs are the property of:

Bourne Co.
Music Publishers
5 West 37th Street
New York, NY 10018

BABY MINE
GIVE A LITTLE WHISTLE
HEIGH-HO
I'VE GOT NO STRINGS
SOME DAY MY PRINCE WILL COME
WHEN YOU WISH UPON A STAR
WHISTLE WHILE YOU WORK
WHO'S AFRAID OF THE BIG BAD WOLF?
WITH A SMILE AND A SONG

Disney Characters and Artwork © Disney Enterprises, Inc.

ISBN 978-1-4950-7740-1

DISTRIBUTED BY

HAL•LEONARD®

7777 W. BLUEMOUND RD. P.O. BOX 13819 MILWAUKEE, WI 53213

For all works contained herein:
Unauthorized copying, arranging, adapting, recording, Internet posting, public performance,
or other distribution of the printed music in this publication is an infringement of copyright.
Infringers are liable under the law.

Visit Hal Leonard Online at
www.halleonard.com

*Based on the "Winnie the Pooh" works,
by A. A. Milne and E. H. Shepard

**TARZAN® Owned by Edgar Rice Burroughs, Inc.
and Used by Permission.
© Burroughs/Disney

Welcome to the *Super Easy Songbook* series!

This unique collection will help you play your favorite songs quickly and easily. Here's how it works:

- Play the simplified melody with your right hand. Letter names appear inside each note to assist you.

- There are no key signatures to worry about! If a sharp ♯ or flat ♭ is needed, it is shown beside the note each time.

- There are no page turns, so your hands never have to leave the keyboard.

- If two notes are connected by a tie ‿, hold the first note for the combined number of beats. (The second note does not show a letter name since it is not re-struck.)

- Add basic chords with your left hand using the provided keyboard diagrams. Chord voicings have been carefully chosen to minimize hand movement.

- The left-hand rhythm is up to you, and chord notes can be played together or separately. Be creative!

- If the chords sound muddy, move your left hand an octave* higher. If this gets in the way of playing the melody, move your right hand an octave higher as well.

    * *An octave spans eight notes. If your starting note is C, the next C to the right is an octave higher.*

–––––––––––––––––––––––– ALSO AVAILABLE ––––––––––––––––––––––––

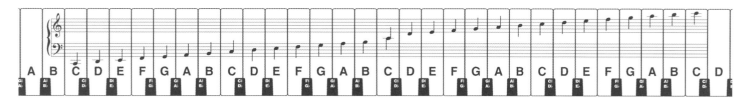

Hal Leonard Student Keyboard Guide HL00296039

Key Stickers HL00100016

(Main Title)
Alice in Wonderland
from ALICE IN WONDERLAND

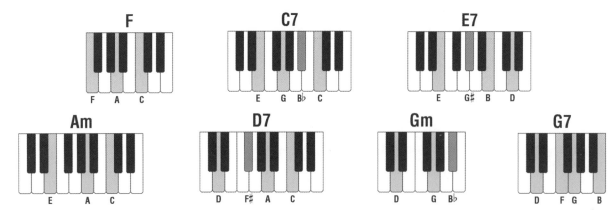

Words by Bob Hilliard
Music by Sammy Fain

Moderately

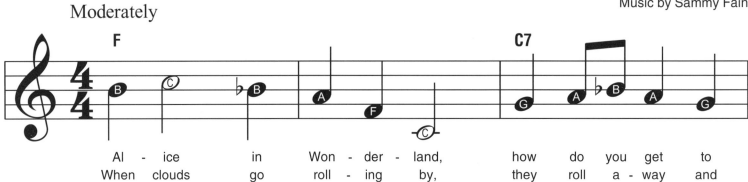

Al - ice in Won - der - land, how do you get to
When clouds go roll - ing by, they roll a - way and

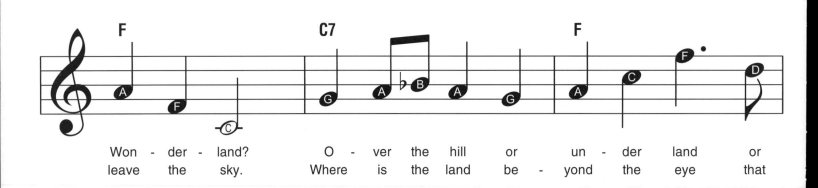

Won - der - land? O - ver the hill or un - der land or
leave the sky. Where is the land be - yond the eye or that

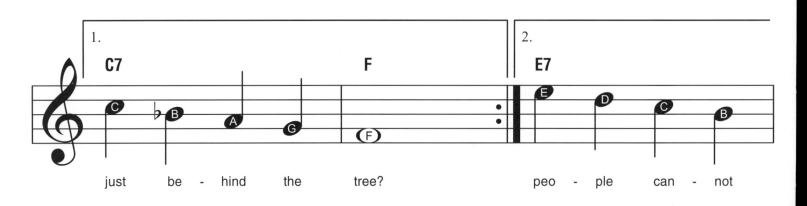

just be - hind the tree? peo - ple can - not

© 1951 Walt Disney Music Company
Copyright Renewed.
All Rights Reserved. Used by Permission.

The Aristocats
from THE ARISTOCATS

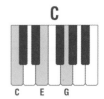
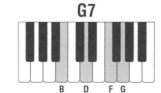
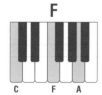

Words and Music by Richard M. Sherman
and Robert B. Sherman

© 1968 Wonderland Music Company, Inc.
Copyright Renewed.
All Rights Reserved. Used by Permission.

Baby Mine

from DUMBO

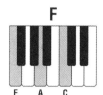 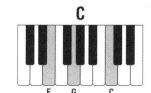 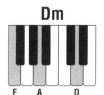 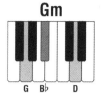

Words by Ned Washington
Music by Frank Churchill

Tenderly

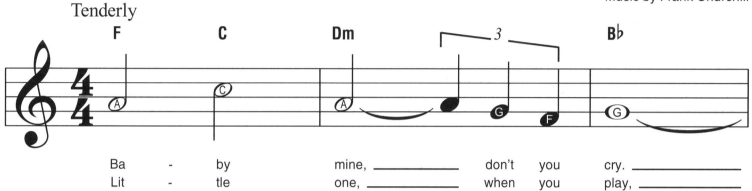

Ba - by mine, _____ don't you cry. _____
Lit - tle one, _____ when you play, _____

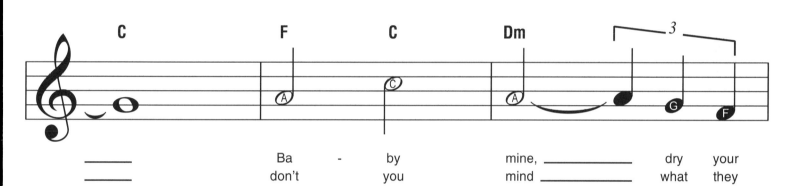

_____ Ba - by mine, _____ dry your
_____ don't you mind _____ what they

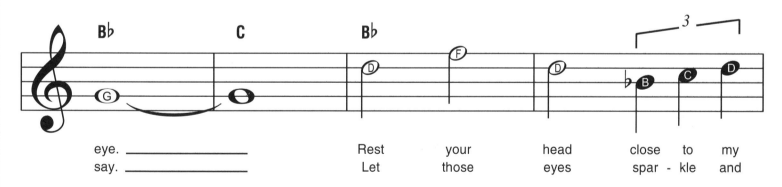

eye. _____ Rest your head close to my
say. _____ Let those eyes spar - kle and

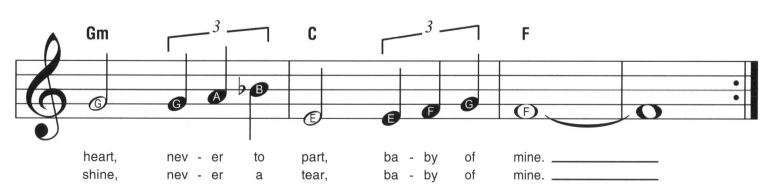

heart, nev - er to part, ba - by of mine. _____
shine, nev - er a tear, ba - by of mine. _____

Copyright © 1941 by Walt Disney Productions
Copyright Renewed.
World Rights Controlled by Bourne Co. (ASCAP)
International Copyright Secured.   All Rights Reserved.

The Ballad of Davy Crockett
from DAVY CROCKETT

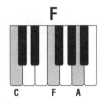
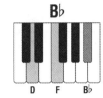
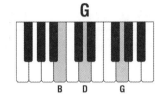
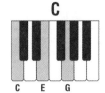

Words by Tom Blackburn
Music by George Bruns

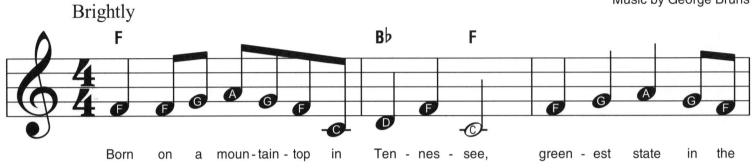

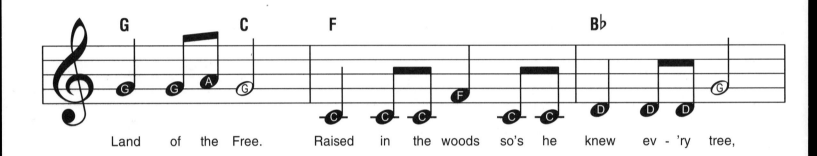

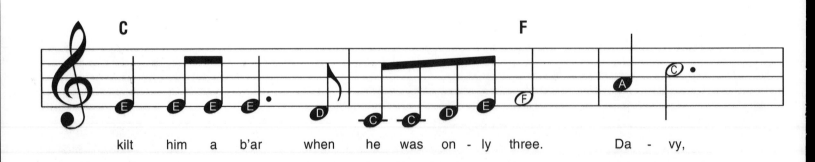

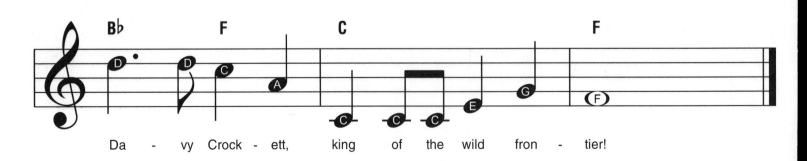

© 1954 Wonderland Music Company, Inc. and Walt Disney Music Company
Copyright Renewed.
All Rights Reserved. Used by Permission.

The Bare Necessities
from THE JUNGLE BOOK

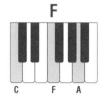 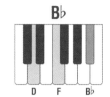 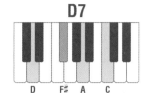 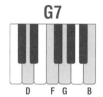 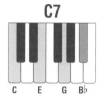

Words and Music by
Terry Gilkyson

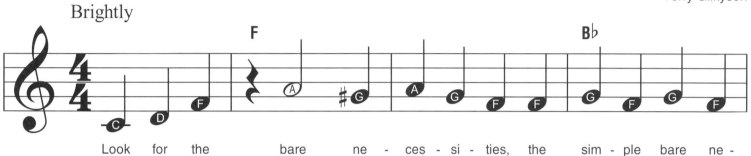

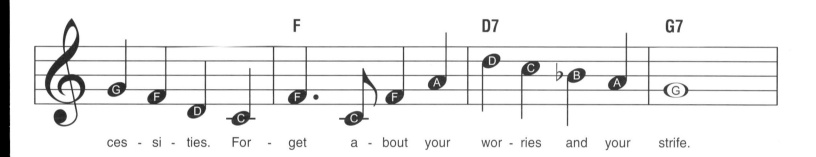

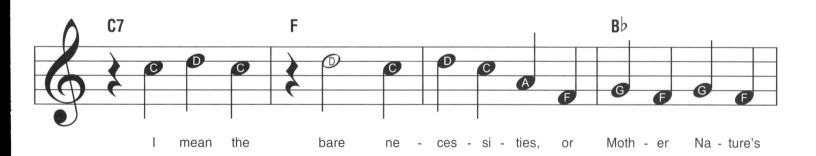

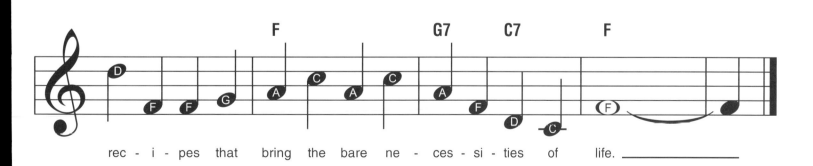

© 1964 Wonderland Music Company, Inc.
Copyright Renewed.
All Rights Reserved. Used by Permission.

Be Our Guest
from BEAUTY AND THE BEAST

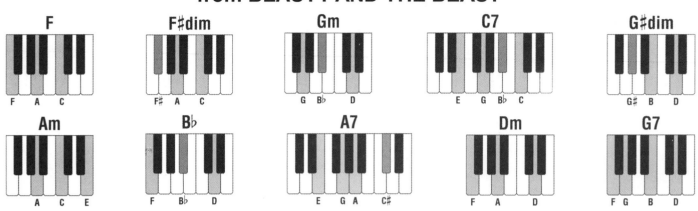

Music by Alan Menken
Lyrics by Howard Ashman

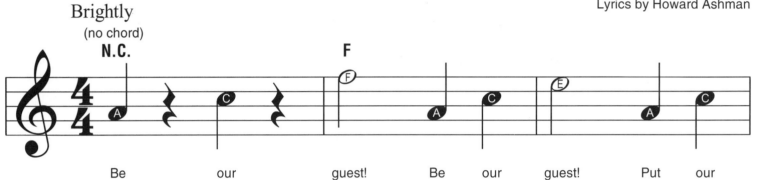

Be our guest! Be our guest! Put our

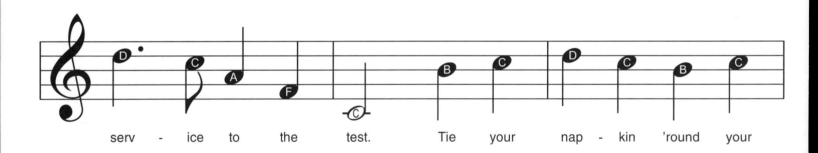

serv - ice to the test. Tie your nap - kin 'round your

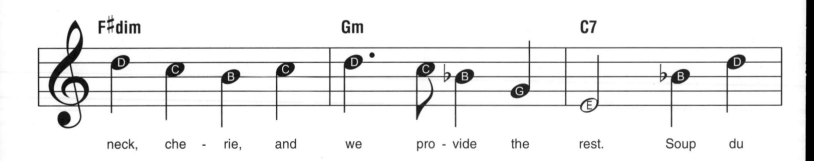

neck, che - rie, and we pro - vide the rest. Soup du

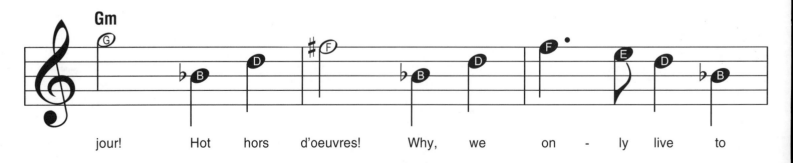

jour! Hot hors d'oeuvres! Why, we on - ly live to

© 1991 Wonderland Music Company, Inc. and Walt Disney Music Company
All Rights Reserved. Used by Permission.

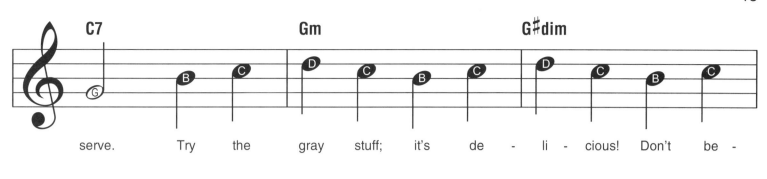

serve.   Try   the   gray   stuff;   it's   de -   li -   cious!   Don't   be -

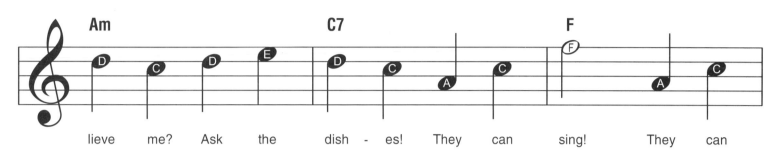

lieve   me?   Ask   the   dish - es!   They   can   sing!   They   can

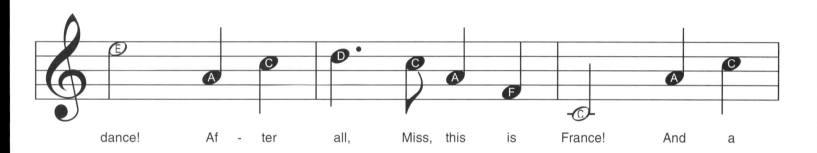

dance!   Af - ter   all,   Miss,   this   is   France!   And   a

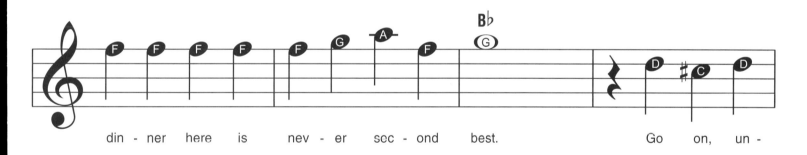

din - ner   here   is   nev - er   sec - ond   best.   Go   on,   un -

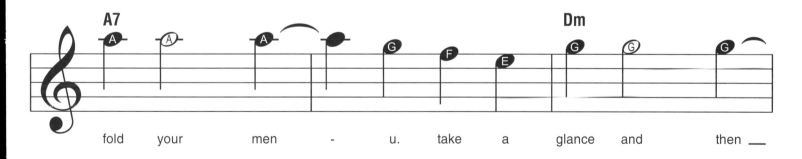

fold   your   men - u.   take   a   glance   and   then __

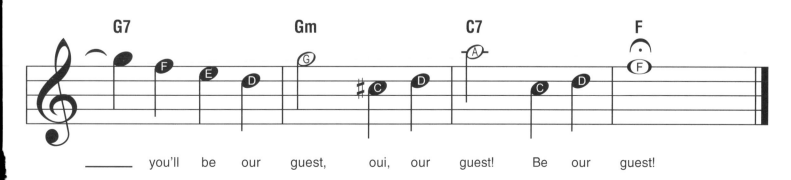

____ you'll   be   our   guest,   oui,   our   guest!   Be   our   guest!

Beauty and the Beast
from BEAUTY AND THE BEAST

Music by Alan Menken
Lyrics by Howard Ashman

© 1991 Wonderland Music Company, Inc. and Walt Disney Music Company
All Rights Reserved. Used by Permission.

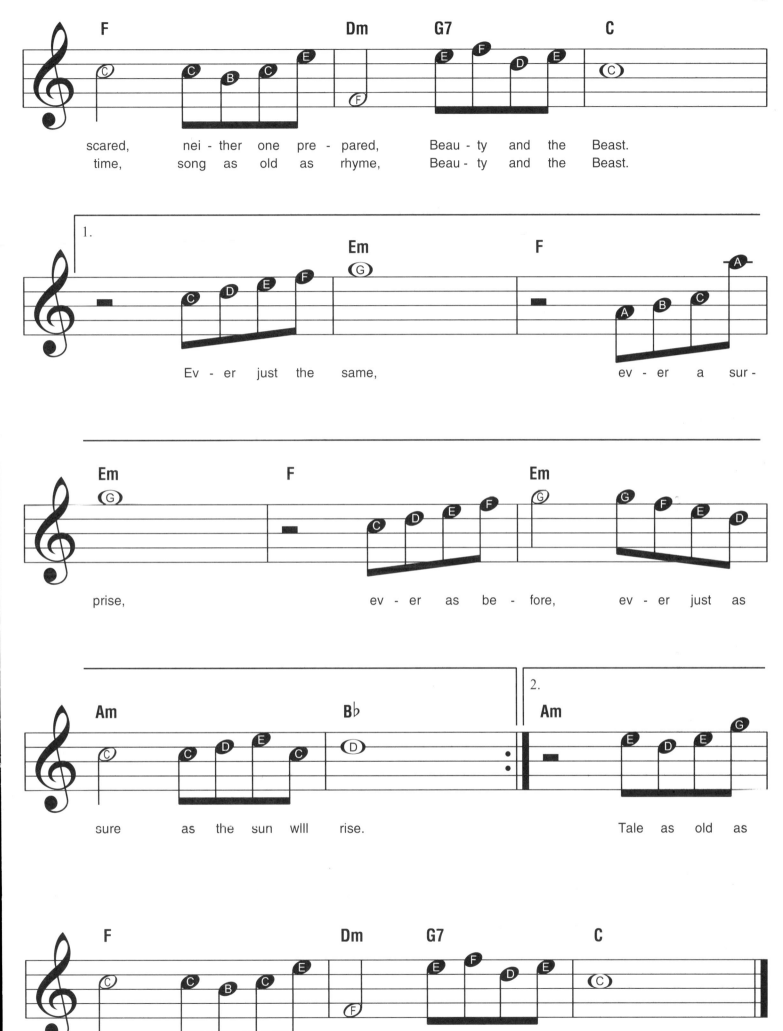

Bella Notte
from LADY AND THE TRAMP

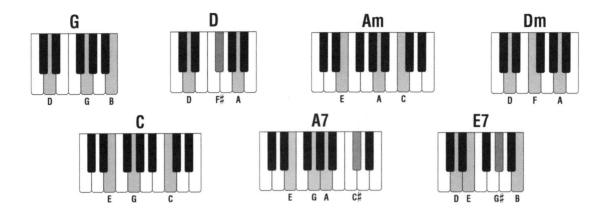

Music and Lyrics by Peggy Lee
and Sonny Burke

Moderately slow

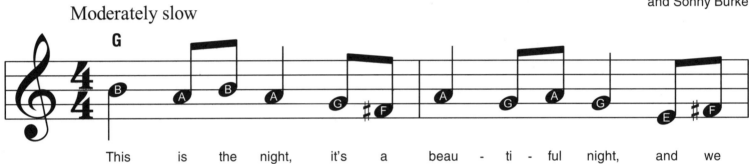

This is the night, it's a beau - ti - ful night, and we

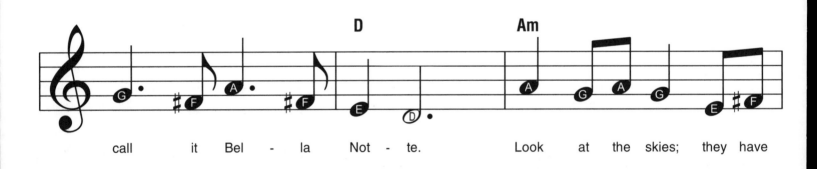

call it Bel - la Not - te. Look at the skies; they have

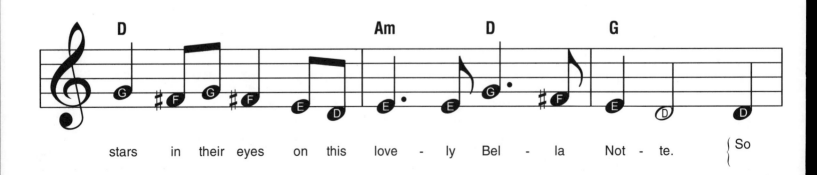

stars in their eyes on this love - ly Bel - la Not - te. { So

© 1952 Walt Disney Music Company
Copyright Renewed.
All Rights Reserved. Used by Permission.

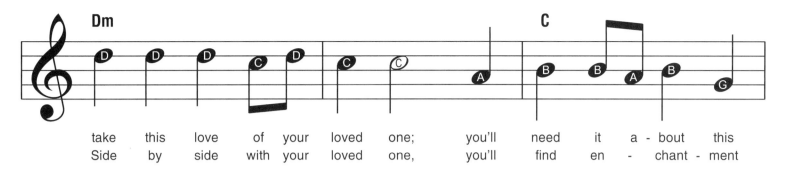

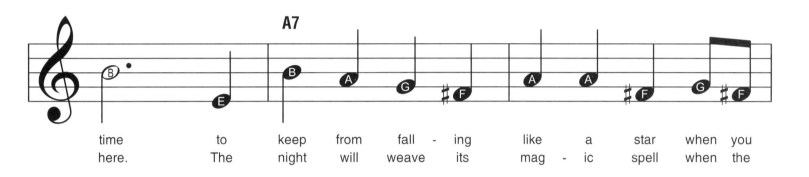

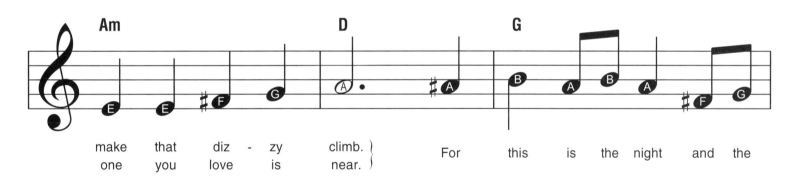

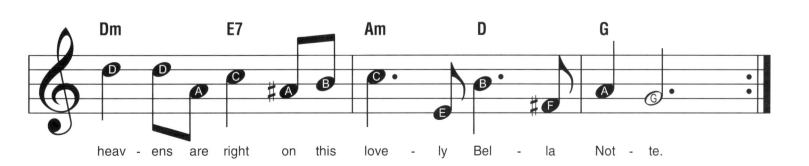

Bibbidi-Bobbidi-Boo
(The Magic Song)
from CINDERELLA

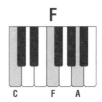 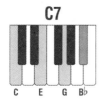 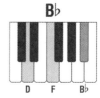 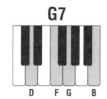

Words by Jerry Livingston
Music by Mack David and Al Hoffman

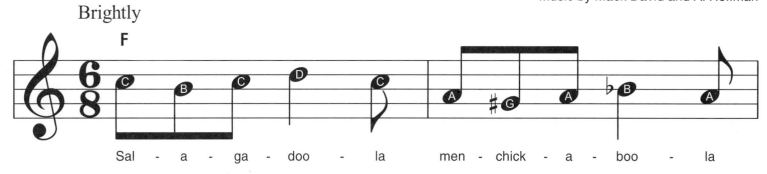

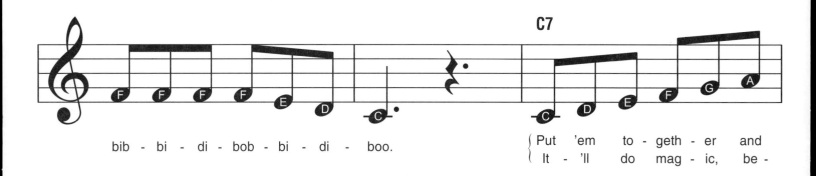

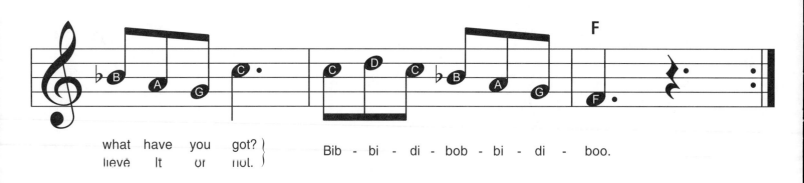

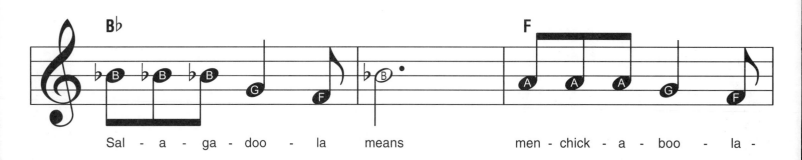

© 1948 Walt Disney Music Company
Copyright Renewed.
All Rights Reserved. Used by Permission.

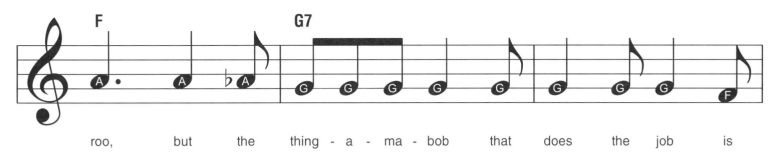

roo,   but   the   thing - a - ma - bob   that   does   the   job   is

bib - bi - di - bob - bi - di - boo.   Sal - a - ga - doo - la

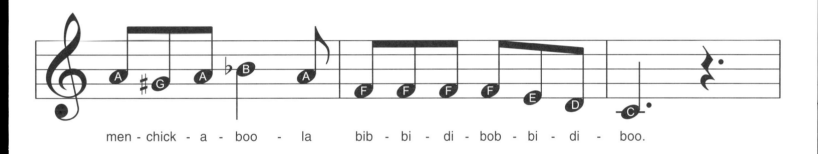

men - chick - a - boo - la   bib - bi - di - bob - bi - di - boo.

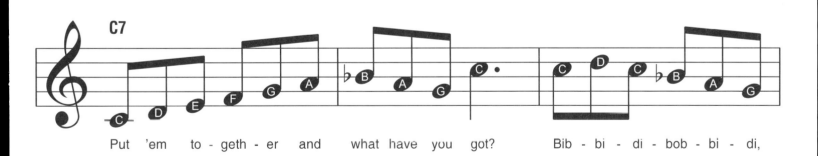

Put 'em to - geth - er   and   what have you got?   Bib - bi - di - bob - bi - di,

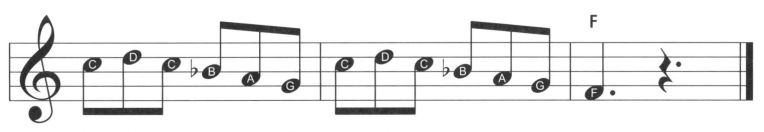

bib - bi - di - bob - bi - di,   bib - bi - di - bob - bi - di - boo.

Can You Feel the Love Tonight
from THE LION KING

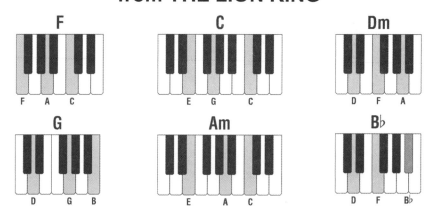

Music by Elton John
Lyrics by Tim Rice

Moderately slow

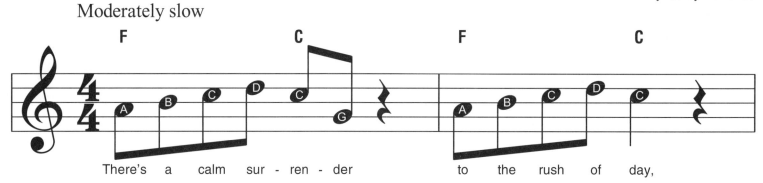

There's a calm sur - ren - der   to the rush of day,

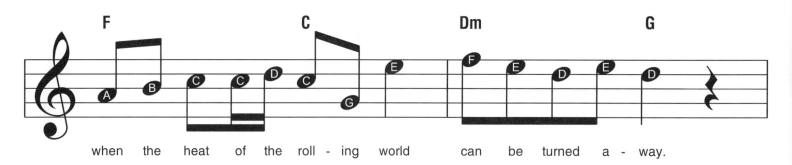

when the heat of the roll - ing world   can be turned a - way.

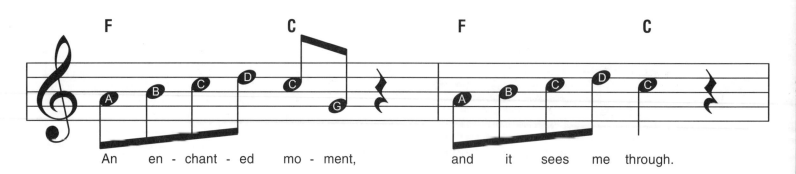

An en - chant - ed mo - ment,   and it sees me through.

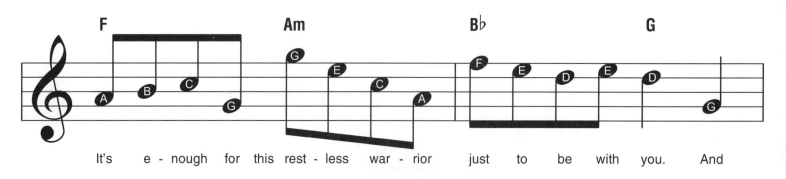

It's e - nough for this rest - less war - rior   just to be with you. And

© 1994 Wonderland Music Company, Inc.
All Rights Reserved. Used by Permission.

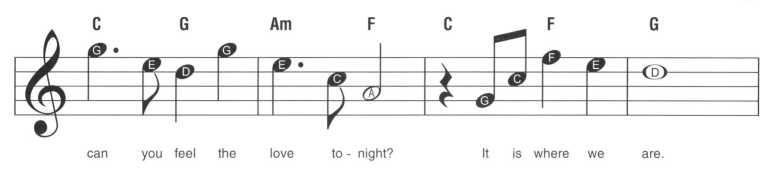

can you feel the love to - night? It is where we are.

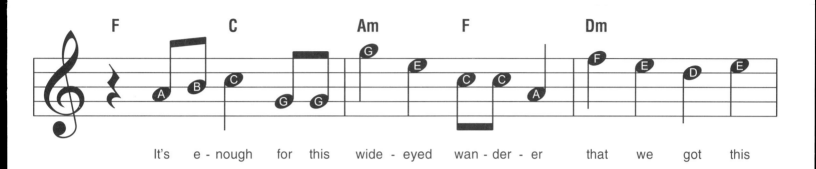

It's e - nough for this wide - eyed wan - der - er that we got this

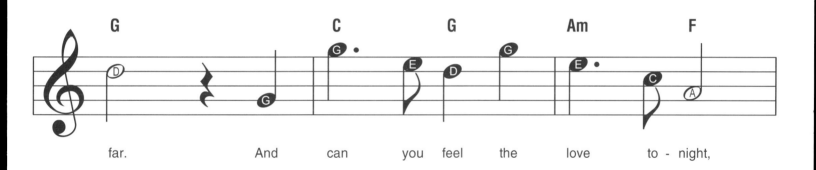

far. And can you feel the love to - night,

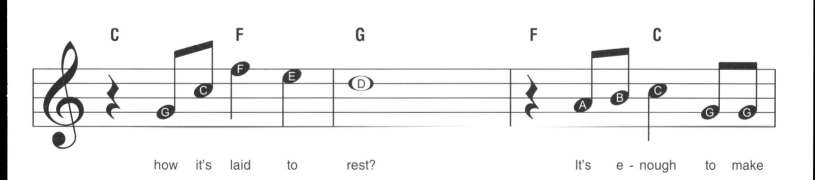

how it's laid to rest? It's e - nough to make

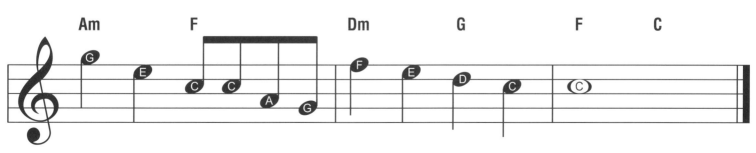

kings and vag - a - bonds be - lieve the ver - y best.

Candle on the Water
from PETE'S DRAGON

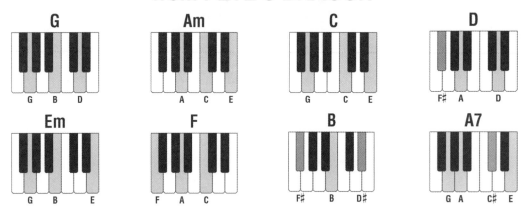

Words and Music by Joel Hirschhorn
and Al Kasha

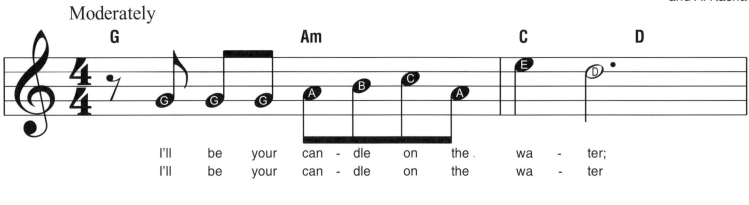

I'll be your can-dle on the wa-ter;
I'll be your can-dle on the wa-ter

my love for you will al-ways burn. I know you're lost and drift-ing,
till ev-'ry wave is warm and bright. My soul is there be-side you;

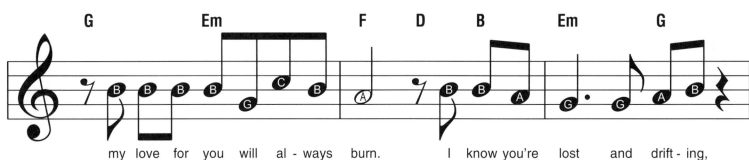

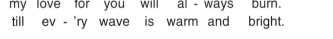

but the clouds are lift-ing. Don't give up; you have some-where to turn.
let this can-dle guide you. Soon you'll see a gold-en stream of light.

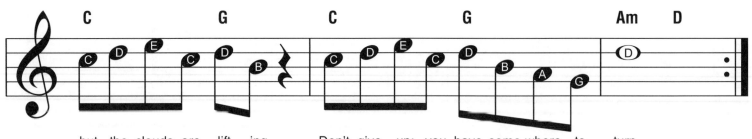

A cold and friend-less tide has found you. Don't let the storm-y dark-ness

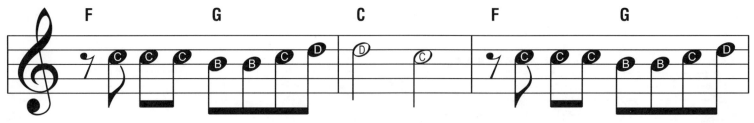

© 1976 Wonderland Music Company, Inc. and Walt Disney Music Company
Copyright Renewed.
All Rights Reserved. Used by Permission.

Chim Chim Cher-ee
from MARY POPPINS

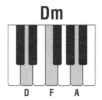 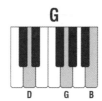 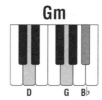 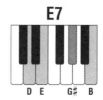 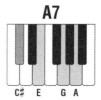

Words and Music by Richard M. Sherman
and Robert B. Sherman

Brightly

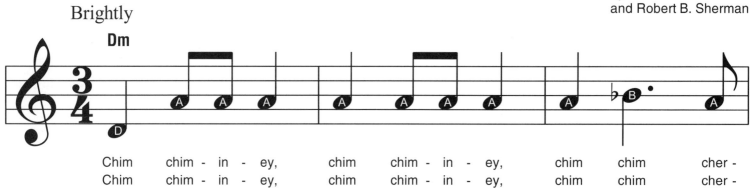

Chim chim - in - ey, chim chim - in - ey, chim chim cher -
Chim chim - in - ey, chim chim - in - ey, chim chim cher -

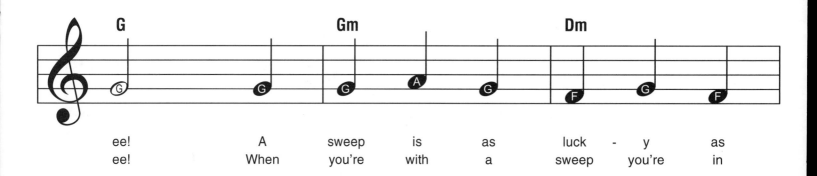

ee! A sweep is as luck - y as
ee! When you're with a sweep you're in

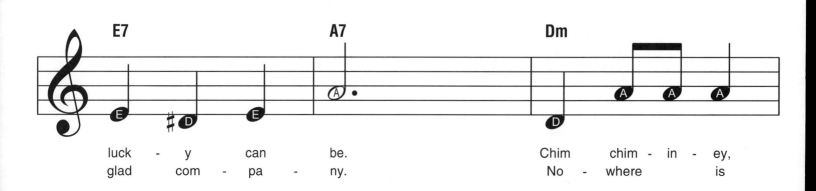

luck - y can be. Chim chim - in - ey,
glad com - pa - ny. No - where is

© 1963 Wonderland Music Company, Inc.
Copyright Renewed.
All Rights Reserved. Used by Permission.

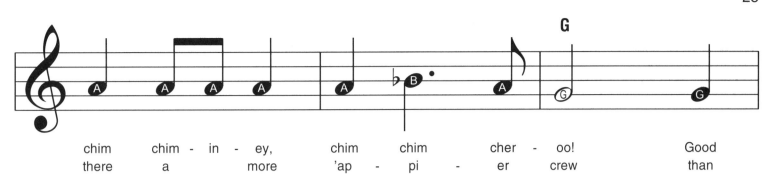

chim   chim - in - ey,   chim   chim   cher - oo!   Good
there   a   more   'ap - pi - er   crew   than

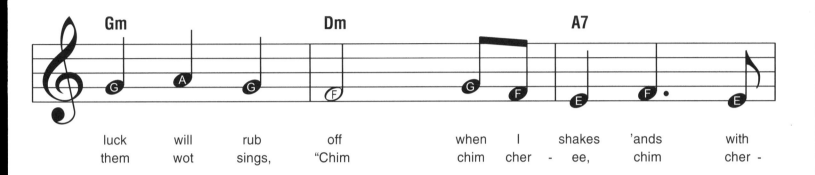

luck   will   rub   off   when   I   shakes   'ands   with
them   wot   sings,   "Chim   chim   cher - ee,   chim   cher -

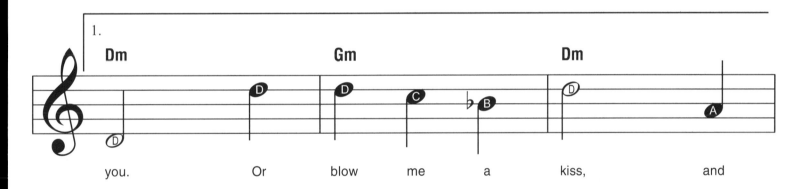

you.   Or   blow   me   a   kiss,   and

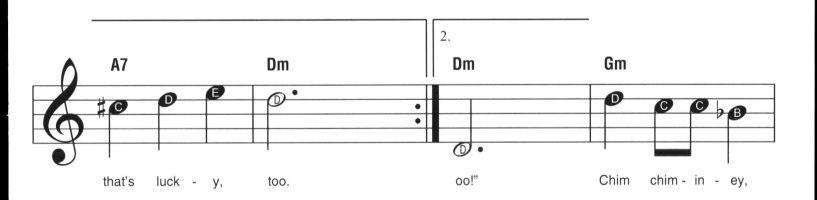

that's   luck - y,   too.   oo!"   Chim   chim - in - ey,

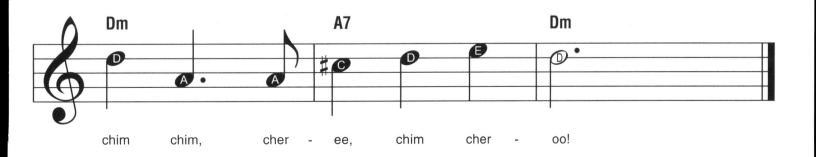

chim   chim,   cher - ee,   chim   cher - oo!

Circle of Life
from THE LION KING

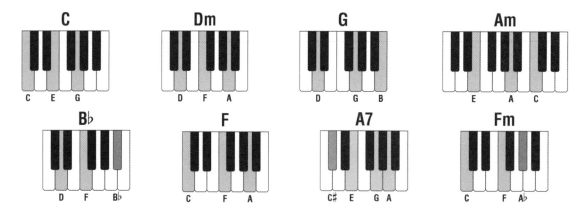

Music by Elton John
Lyrics by Tim Rice

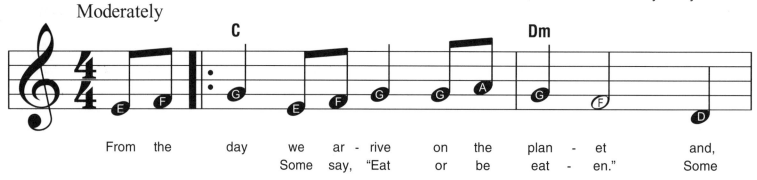

From the day we ar-rive on the plan-et and,
Some say, "Eat or be eat-en." Some

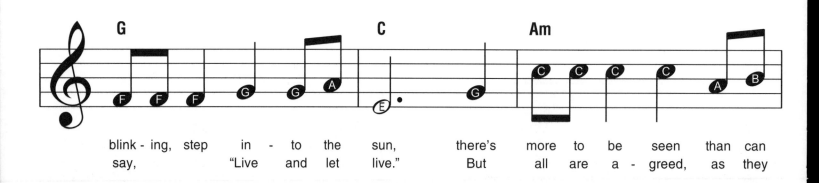

blink-ing, step in-to the sun, there's more to be seen than can
say, "Live and let live." But all are a-greed, as they

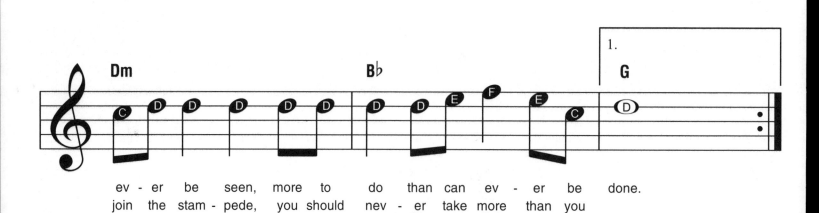

ev-er be seen, more to do than can ev-er be done.
join the stam-pede, you should nev-er take more than you

© 1994 Wonderland Music Company, Inc.
All Rights Reserved. Used by Permission.

Colors of the Wind
from POCAHONTAS

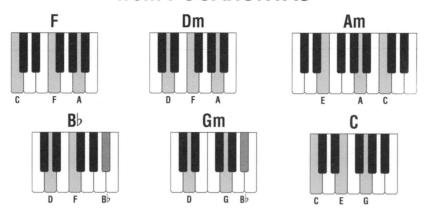

Music by Alan Menken
Lyrics by Stephen Schwartz

Moderately

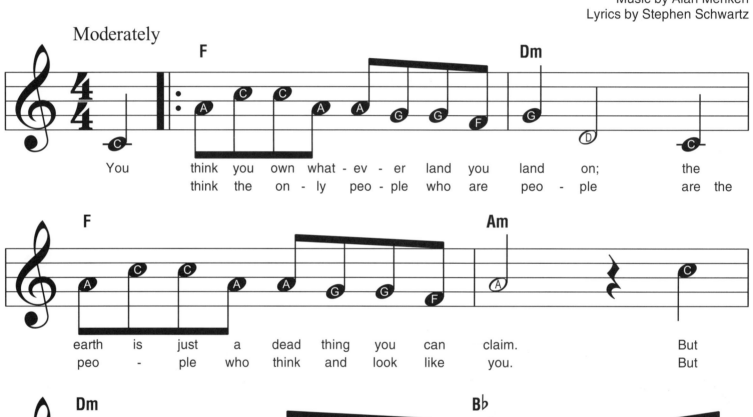

You think you own what-ev-er land you land on; the
think the on-ly peo-ple who are peo-ple are the

earth is just a dead thing you can claim. But
peo-ple who think and look like you. But

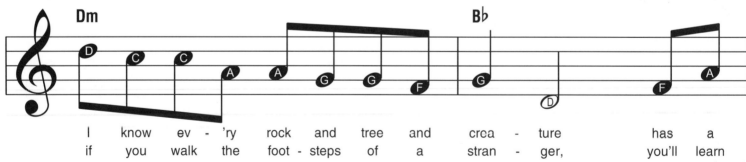

I know ev-'ry rock and tree and crea-ture, has a
if you walk the foot-steps of a stran-ger, you'll learn

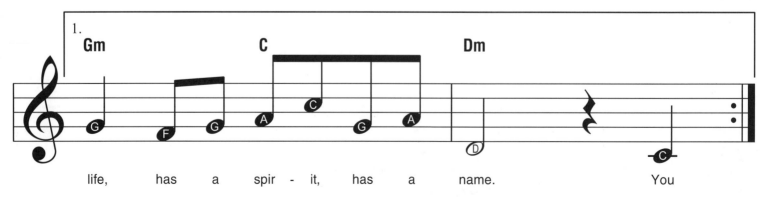

life, has a spir-it, has a name. You

© 1995 Wonderland Music Company, Inc. and Walt Disney Music Company
All Rights Reserved. Used by Permission.

Do You Want to Build a Snowman?

from FROZEN

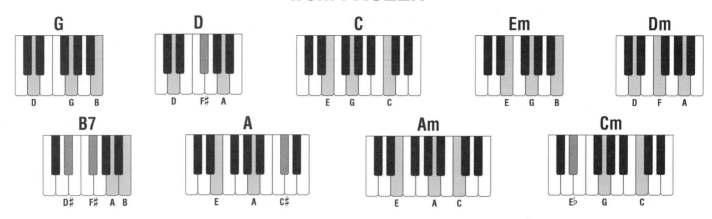

Music and Lyrics by Kristen Anderson-Lopez
and Robert Lopez

Brightly

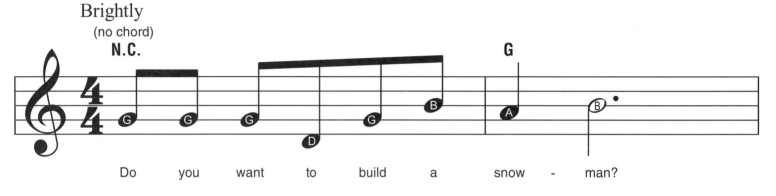

Do you want to build a snow - man?

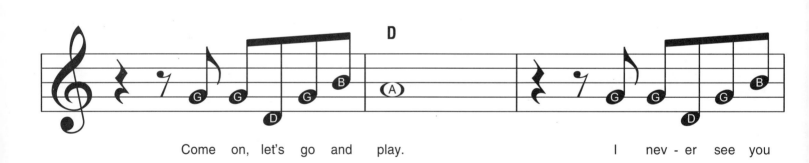

Come on, let's go and play. I nev - er see you

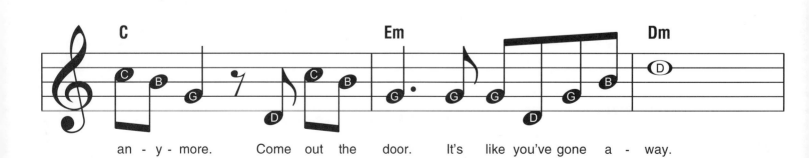

an - y - more. Come out the door. It's like you've gone a - way.

© 2013 Wonderland Music Company, Inc.
All Rights Reserved. Used by Permission.

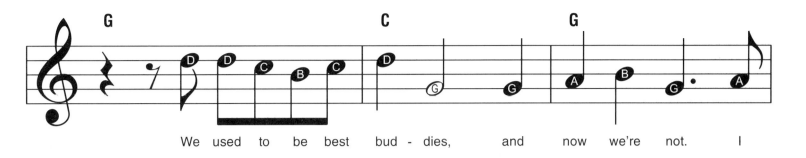

We used to be best bud - dies, and now we're not. I

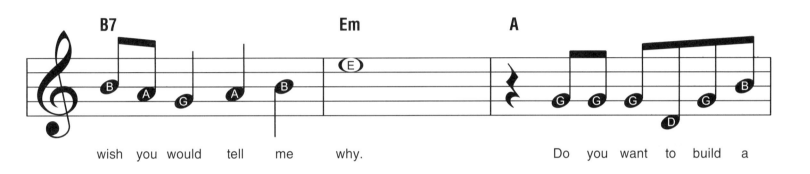

wish you would tell me why. Do you want to build a

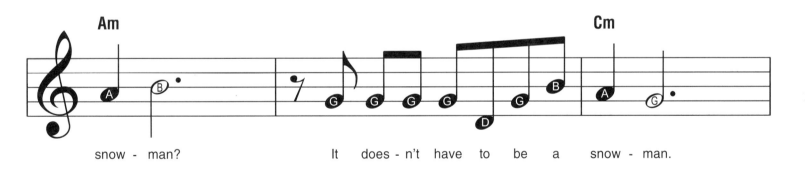

snow - man? It does - n't have to be a snow - man.

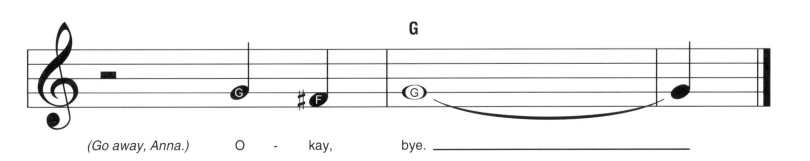

(Go away, Anna.) O - kay, bye. _____

A Dream Is a Wish Your Heart Makes

from CINDERELLA

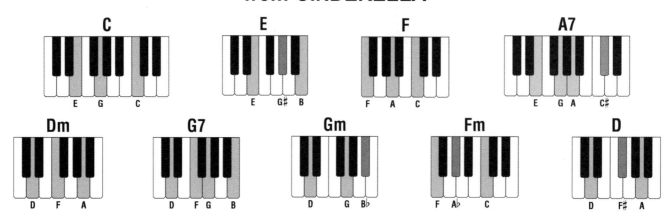

Words and Music by Mack David,
Al Hoffman and Jerry Livingston

Moderately fast

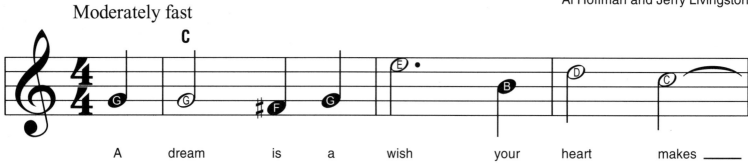

A dream is a wish your heart makes _____

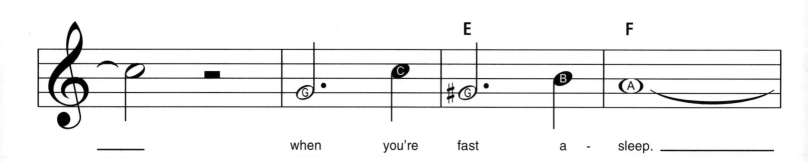

_____ when you're fast a - sleep. _____

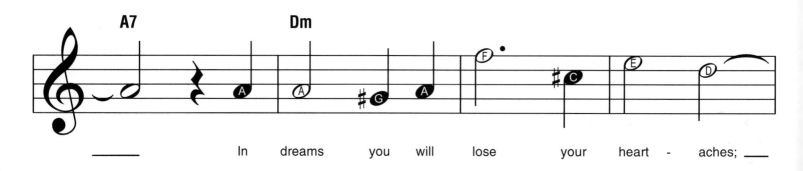

_____ In dreams you will lose your heart - aches; _____

© 1948 Walt Disney Music Company
Copyright Renewed.
All Rights Reserved. Used by Permission.

Friend Like Me
from ALADDIN

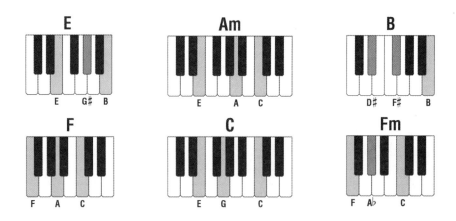

Music by Alan Menken
Lyrics by Howard Ashman

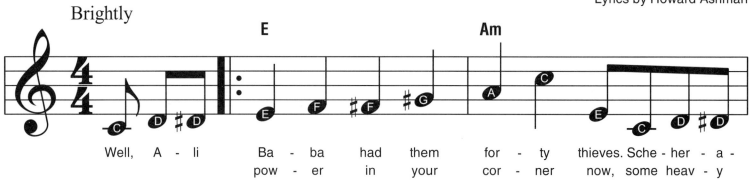

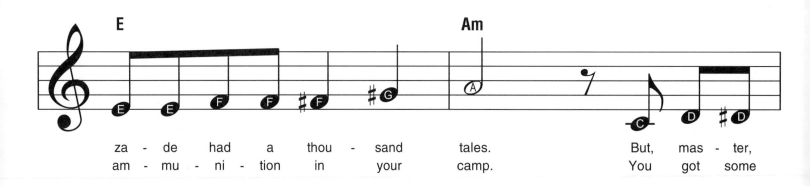

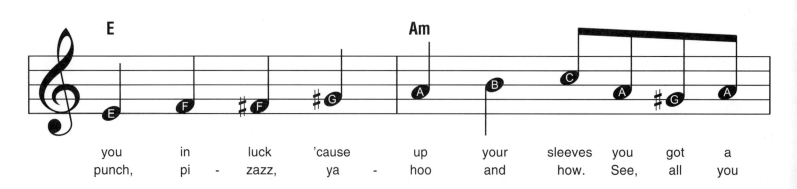

© 1992 Wonderland Music Company, Inc. and Walt Disney Music Company
All Rights Reserved. Used by Permission.

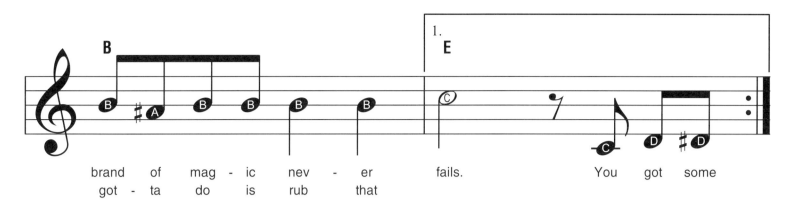

brand of mag - ic nev - er fails. You got some
got - ta do is rub that

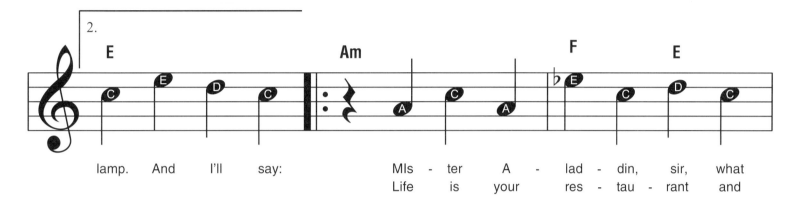

lamp. And I'll say: MIs - ter A - lad - din, sir, what
Life is your res - tau - rant and

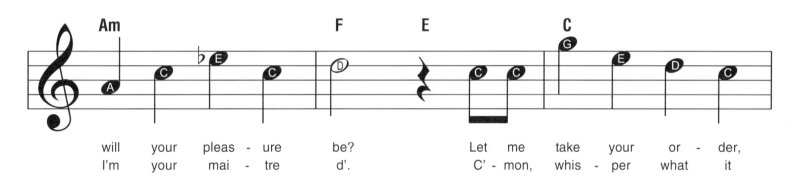

will your pleas - ure be? Let me take your or - der,
I'm your mai - tre d'. C' - mon, whis - per what it

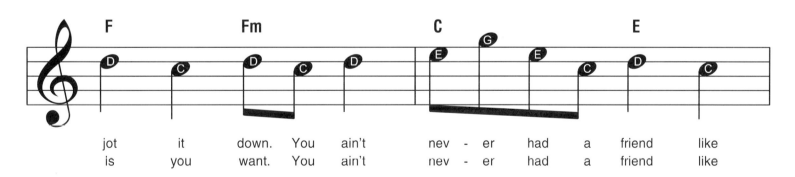

jot it down. You ain't nev - er had a friend like
is you want. You ain't nev - er had a friend like

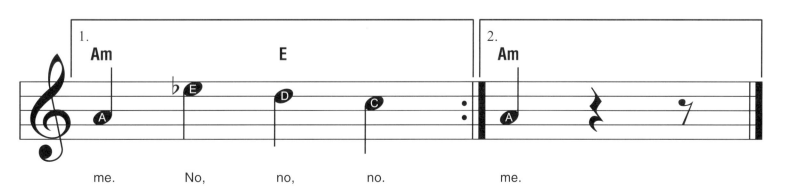

me. No, no, no. me.

Give a Little Whistle
from PINOCCHIO

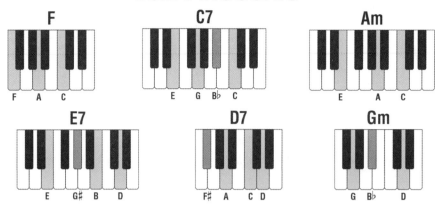

Words by Ned Washington
Music by Leigh Harline

Brightly

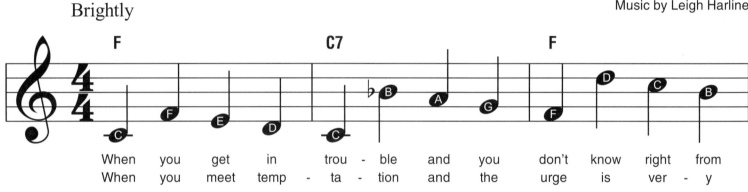

When you get in trou - ble and you don't know right from
When you meet temp - ta - tion and the urge is ver - y

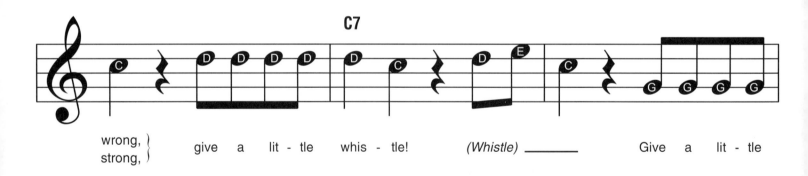

wrong, } give a lit - tle whis - tle! (Whistle) _____ Give a lit - tle
strong, }

whis - tle! (Whistle) _____ Not just a

Copyright © 1940 by Bourne Co. (ASCAP)
Copyright Renewed.
International Copyright Secured. All Rights Reserved.

Go the Distance
from HERCULES

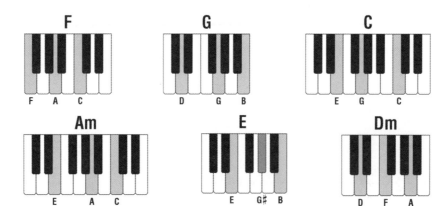

Music by Alan Menken
Lyrics by David Zippel

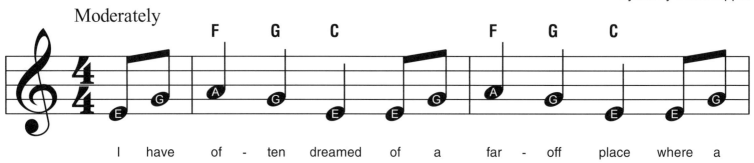

I have of - ten dreamed of a far - off place where a

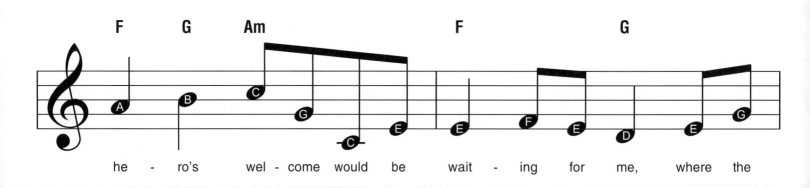

he - ro's wel - come would be wait - ing for me, where the

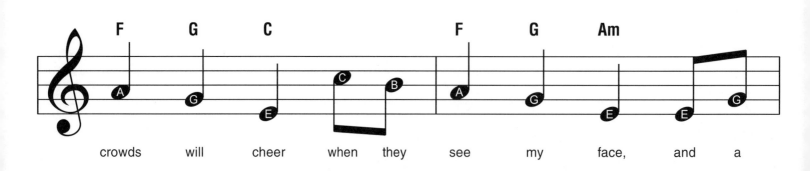

crowds will cheer when they see my face, and a

© 1997 Wonderland Music Company, Inc. and Walt Disney Music Company
All Rights Reserved. Used by Permission.

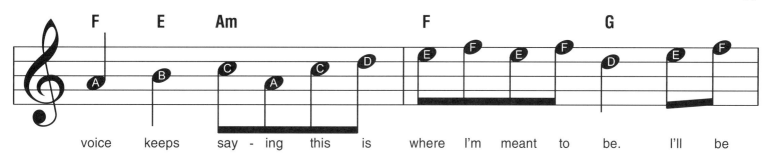

voice keeps say - ing this is where I'm meant to be. I'll be

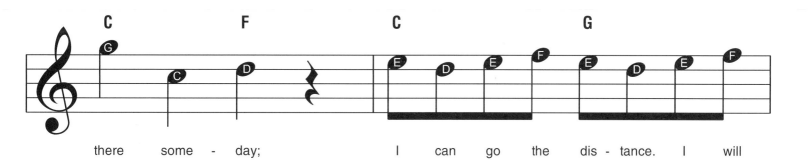

there some - day; I can go the dis - tance. I will

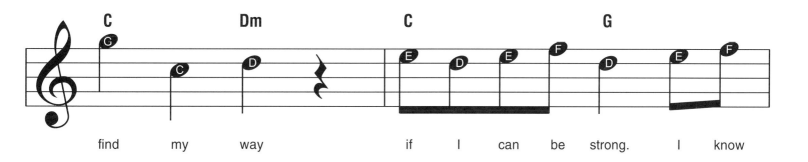

find my way if I can be strong. I know

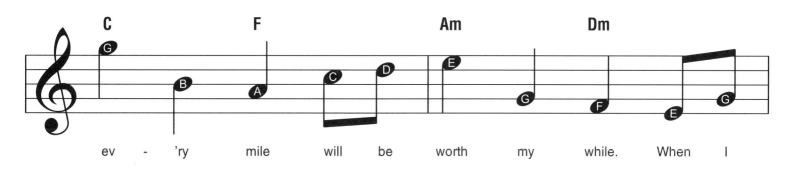

ev - 'ry mile will be worth my while. When I

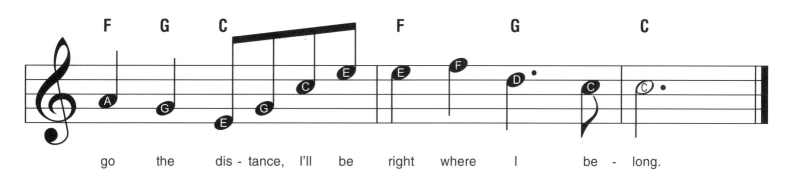

go the dis - tance, I'll be right where I be - long.

God Help the Outcasts
from THE HUNCHBACK OF NOTRE DAME

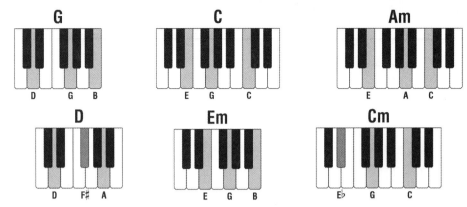

Music by Alan Menken
Lyrics by Stephen Schwartz

Prayerfully

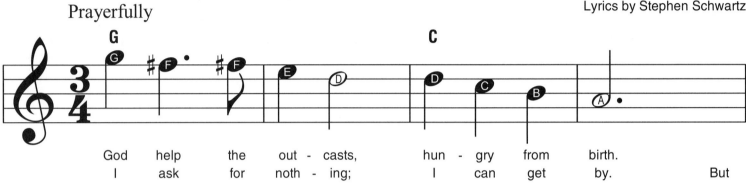

God help the out-casts, hun-gry from birth.
I ask for noth-ing; I can get by. But

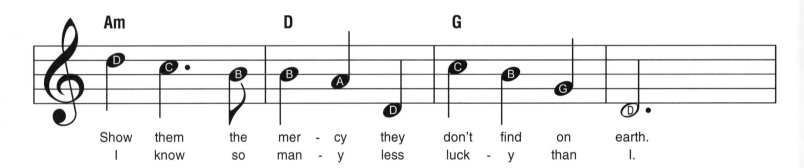

Show them the mer-cy they don't find on earth.
I know so man-y less luck-y than I.

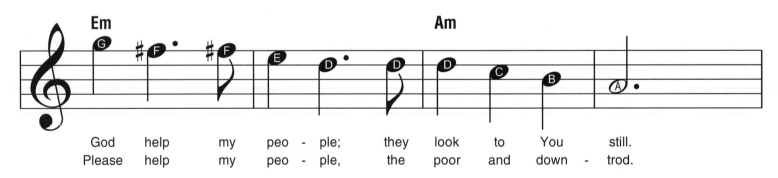

God help my peo-ple; they look to You still.
Please help my peo-ple, the poor and down-trod.

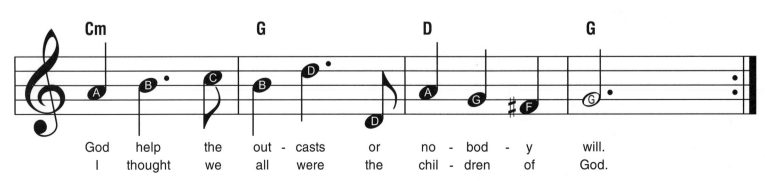

God help the out-casts or no-bod-y will.
I thought we all were the chil-dren of God.

© 1996 Wonderland Music Company, Inc. and Walt Disney Music Company
All Rights Reserved. Used by Permission.

Heigh-Ho
The Dwarfs' Marching Song from SNOW WHITE AND THE SEVEN DWARFS

Words by Larry Morey
Music by Frank Churchill

Copyright © 1937 by Bourne Co. (ASCAP)
Copyright Renewed.
International Copyright Secured.   All Rights Reserved.

Hakuna Matata
from THE LION KING

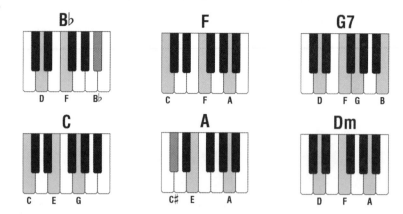

Music by Elton John
Lyrics by Tim Rice

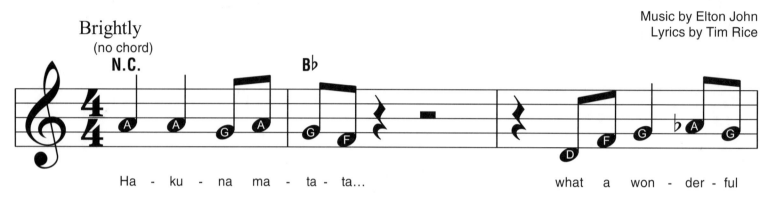

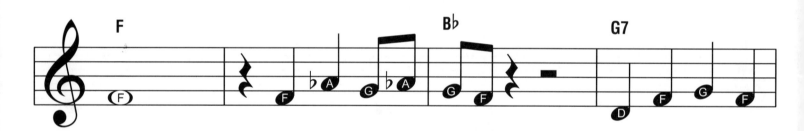

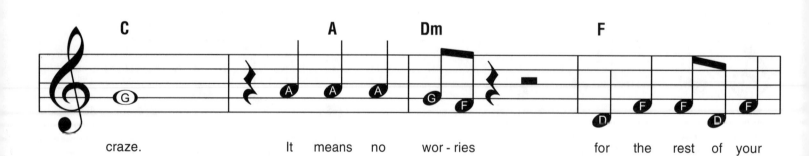

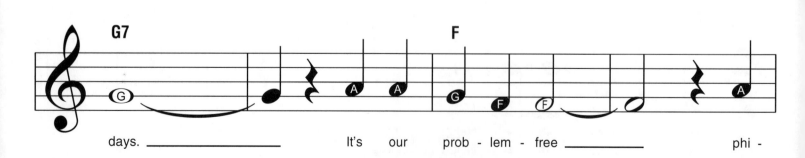

© 1994 Wonderland Music Company, Inc.
All Rights Reserved. Used by Permission.

43

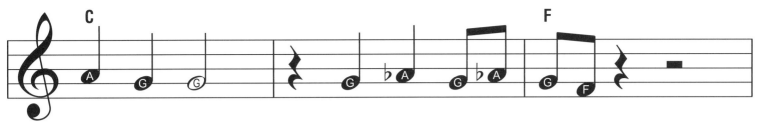

los - o - phy.   Ha - ku - na ma - ta - ta.

Ha - ku - na ma - ta - ta...   what a won - der - ful

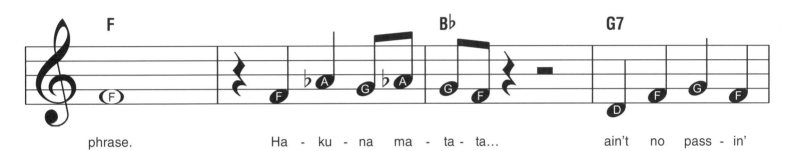

phrase.   Ha - ku - na ma - ta - ta...   ain't no pass - in'

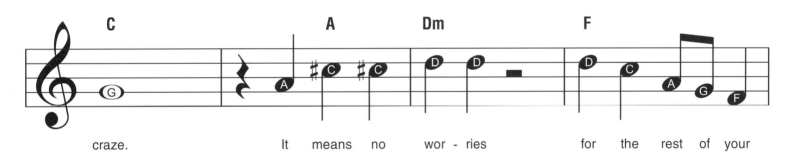

craze.   It means no wor - ries   for the rest of your

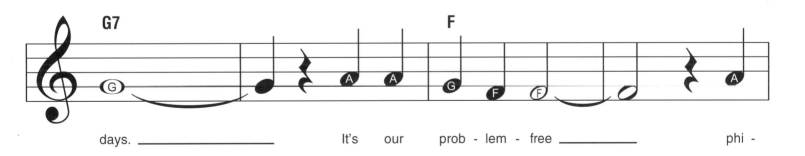

days. _____   It's our prob - lem - free _____ phi -

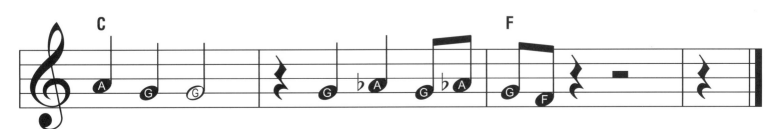

los - o - phy.   Ha - ku - na ma - ta - ta.

He's a Tramp
from LADY AND THE TRAMP

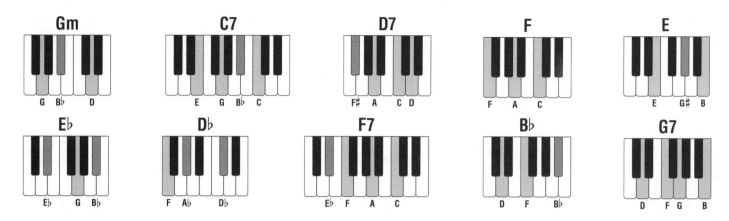

Words and Music by Peggy Lee
and Sonny Burke

Moderate Shuffle

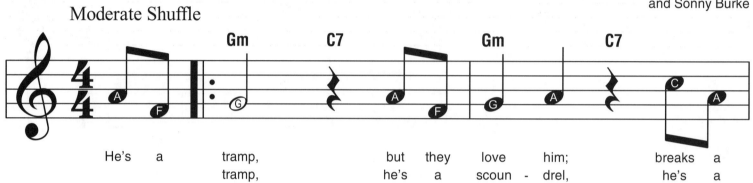

He's a tramp, but they love him; breaks a
tramp, he's a love scoun - drel, he's a

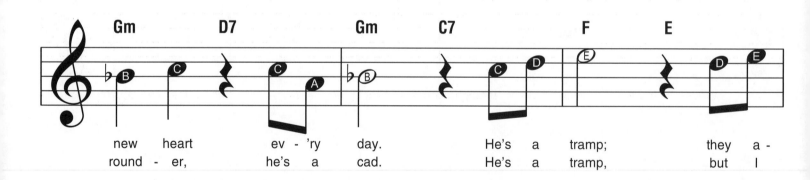

new heart ev - 'ry day. He's a tramp; they a -
round - er, he's a cad. He's a tramp, but I

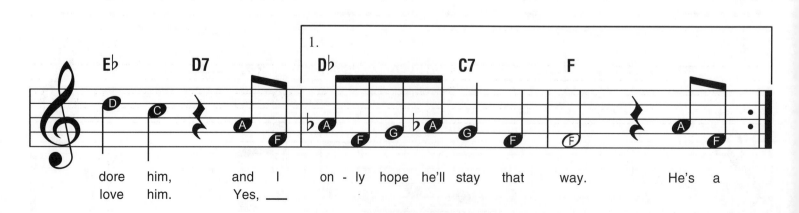

dore him, and I on - ly hope he'll stay that way. He's a
love him. Yes, ___

© 1952 Walt Disney Music Company
Copyright Renewed.
All Rights Reserved. Used by Permission.

I See the Light

from TANGLED

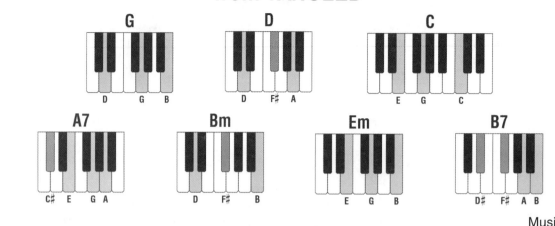

Music by Alan Menken
Lyrics by Glenn Slater

Moderately

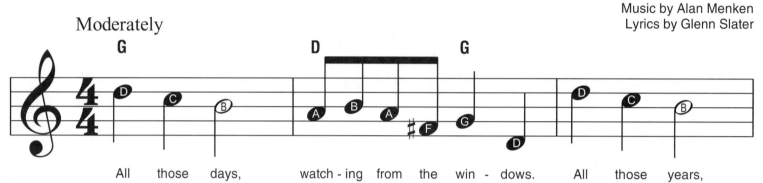

All those days, watch-ing from the win-dows. All those years,

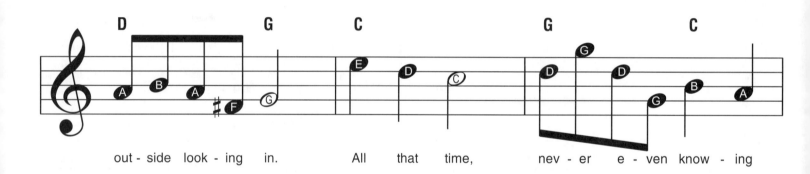

out-side look-ing in. All that time, nev-er e-ven know-ing

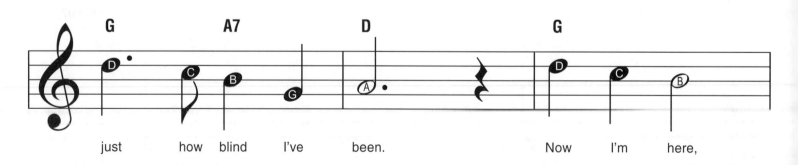

just how blind I've been. Now I'm here,

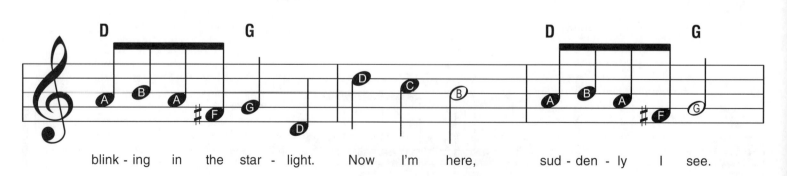

blink-ing in the star-light. Now I'm here, sud-den-ly I see.

© 2010 Wonderland Music Company, Inc. and Walt Disney Music Company
All Rights Reserved. Used by Permission.

I've Got No Strings

from PINOCCHIO

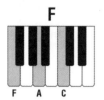
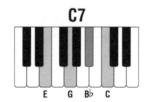
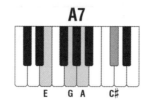
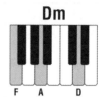

Words by Ned Washington
Music by Leigh Harline

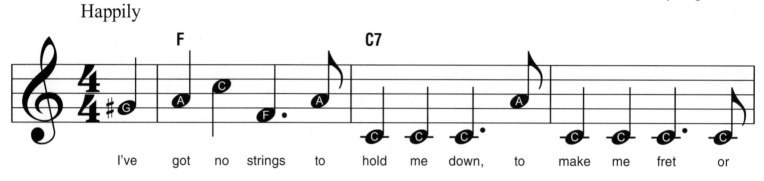

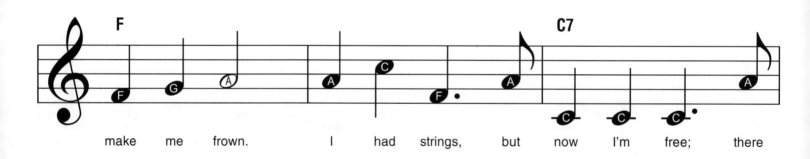

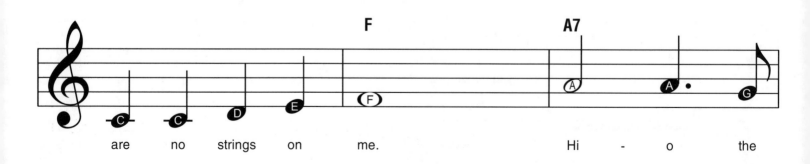

Copyright © 1940 by Bourne Co. (ASCAP)
Copyright Renewed.
International Copyright Secured.   All Rights Reserved.

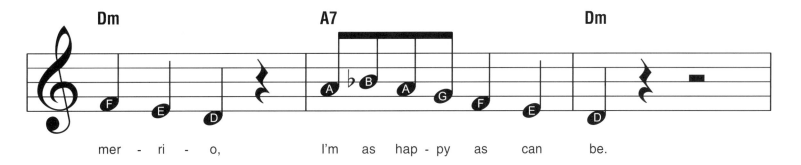

mer - ri - o, I'm as hap - py as can be.

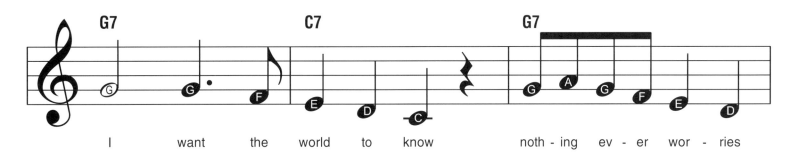

I want the world to know noth - ing ev - er wor - ries

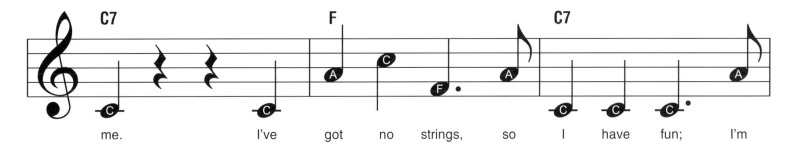

me. I've got no strings, so I have fun; I'm

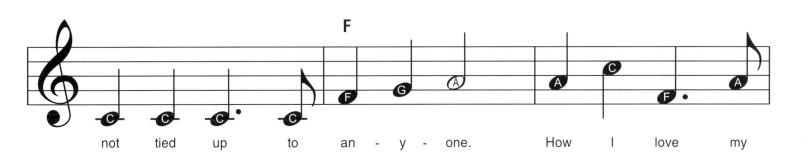

not tied up to an - y - one. How I love my

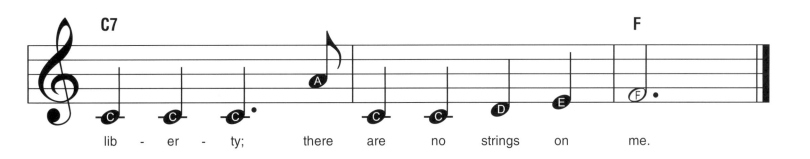

lib - er - ty; there are no strings on me.

If I Never Knew You
(End Title)
from POCAHONTAS

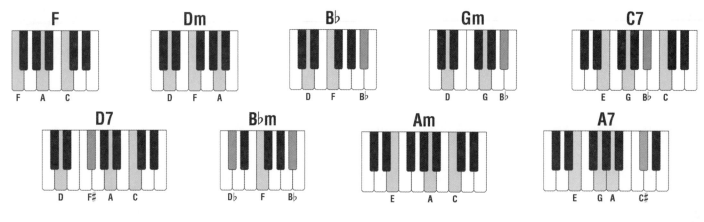

Music by Alan Menken
Lyrics by Stephen Schwartz

Moderately slow

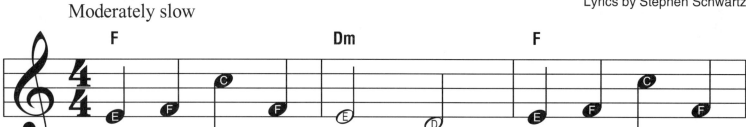

If I nev - er knew you, if I nev - er

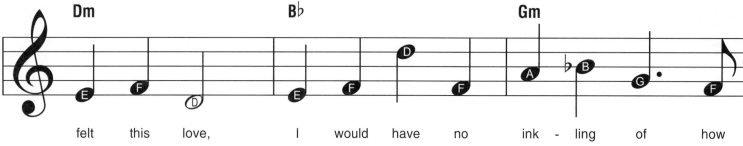

felt this love, I would have no ink - ling of how

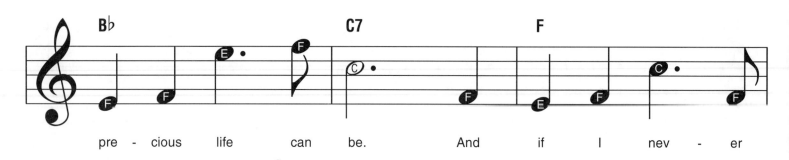

pre - cious life can be. And if I nev - er

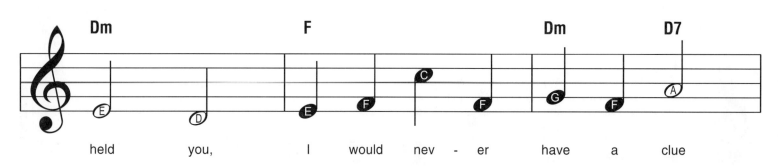

held you, I would nev - er have a clue

© 1995 Wonderland Music Company, Inc. and Walt Disney Music Company
All Rights Reserved. Used by Permission.

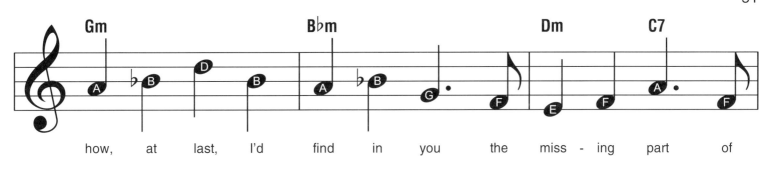

how, at last, I'd find in you the miss - ing part of

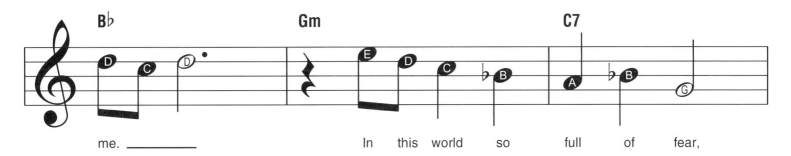

me. _____ In this world so full of fear,

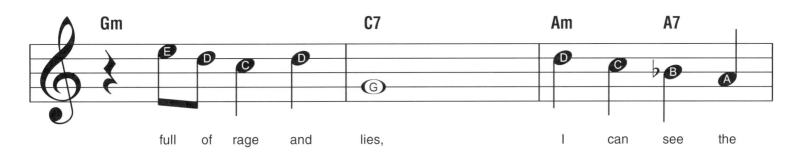

full of rage and lies, I can see the

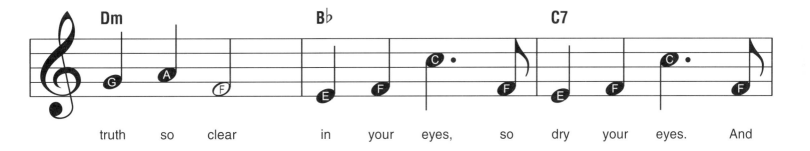

truth so clear in your eyes, so dry your eyes. And

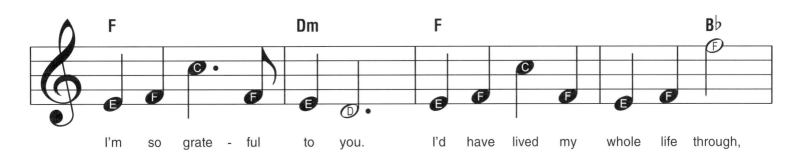

I'm so grate - ful to you. I'd have lived my whole life through,

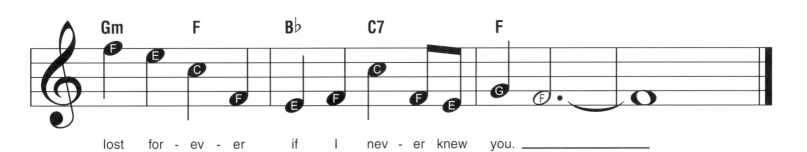

lost for - ev - er if I nev - er knew you. _____

It's a Small World

from Disneyland Resort® and Magic Kingdom® Park

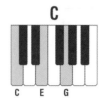 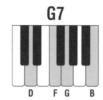 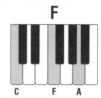 

Words and Music by Richard M. Sherman
and Robert B. Sherman

Brightly

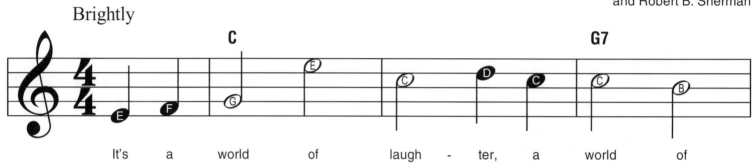

It's a world of laugh - ter, a world of

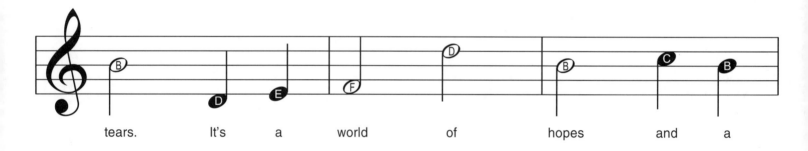

tears. It's a world of hopes and a

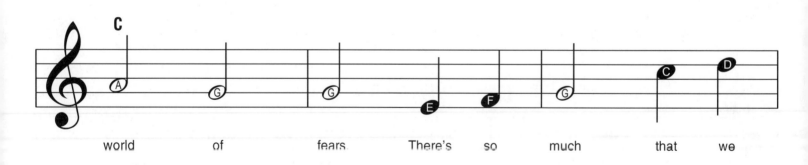

world of fears. There's so much that we

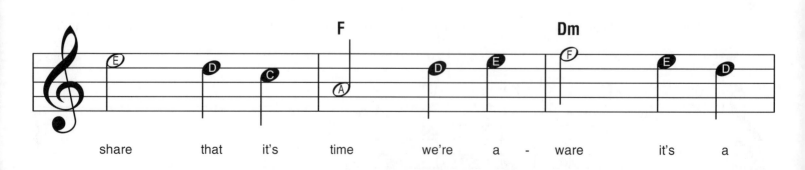

share that it's time we're a - ware it's a

© 1963 Wonderland Music Company, Inc.
Copyright Renewed.
All Rights Reserved. Used by Permission.

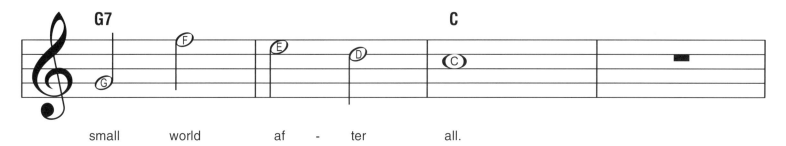

small   world   af - ter   all.

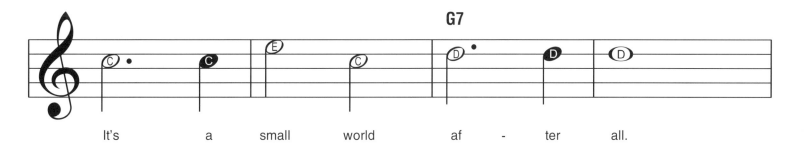

It's   a   small   world   af - ter   all.

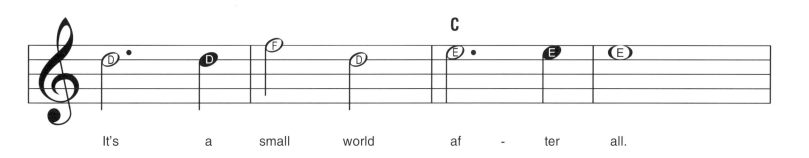

It's   a   small   world   af - ter   all.

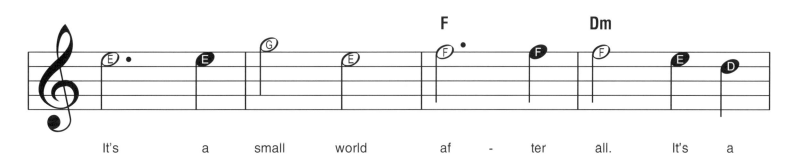

It's   a   small   world   af - ter   all.   It's   a

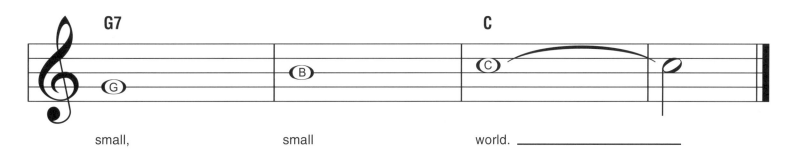

small,   small   world. _____

Kiss the Girl
from THE LITTLE MERMAID

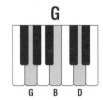
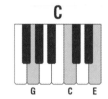

Music by Alan Menken
Lyrics by Howard Ashman

Moderately

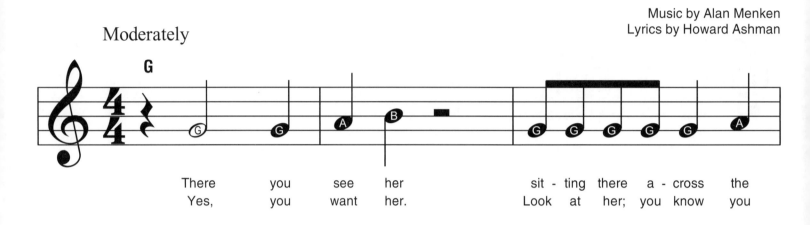

There you see her sit - ting there a - cross the
Yes, you want her. Look at her; you know you

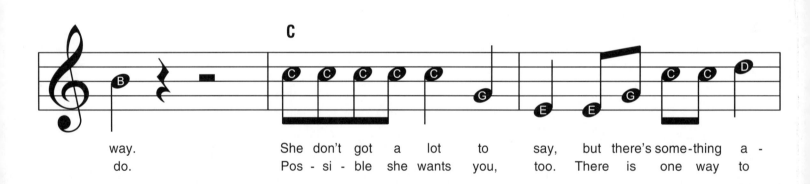

way. She don't got a lot to say, but there's some-thing a -
do. Pos - si - ble she wants you, too. There is one way to

bout her. And you don't know why, but you're
ask her. It don't take a word, not a

© 1988 Wonderland Music Company, Inc. and Walt Disney Music Company
All Rights Reserved. Used by Permission.

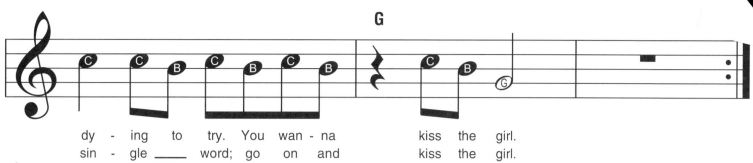

dy - ing to try. You wan - na kiss the girl.
sin - gle ___ word; go on and kiss the girl.

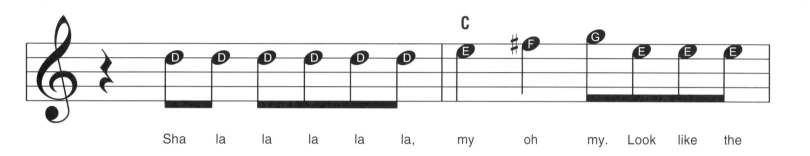

Sha la la la la la, my oh my. Look like the

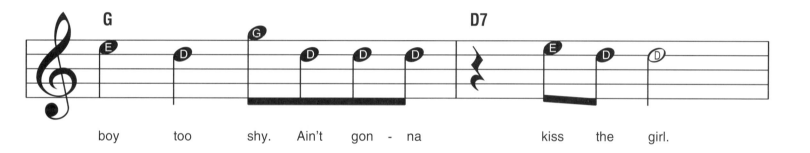

boy too shy. Ain't gon - na kiss the girl.

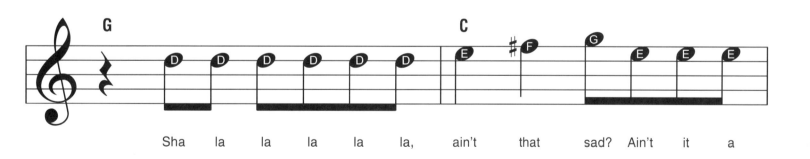

Sha la la la la la, ain't that sad? Ain't it a

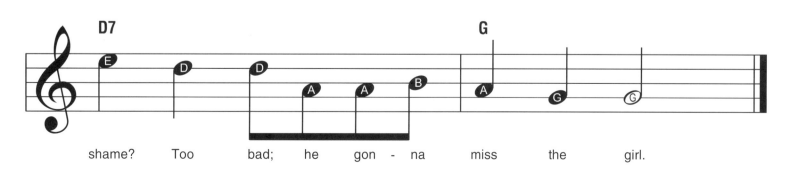

shame? Too bad; he gon - na miss the girl.

Lava
from LAVA

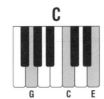
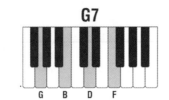
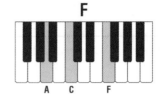

Music and Lyrics by
James Ford Murphy

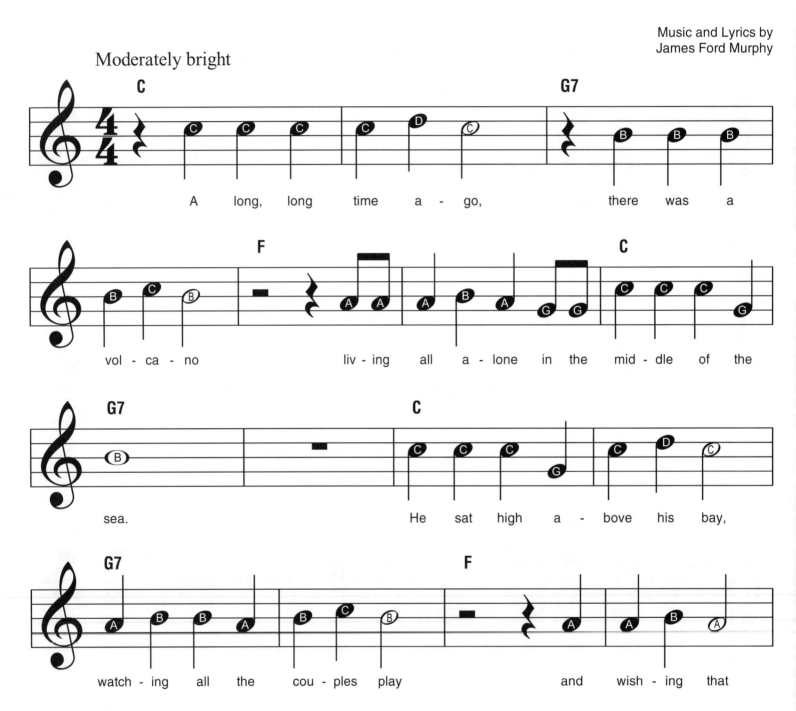

Moderately bright

A long, long time a - go, there was a vol - ca - no liv - ing all a - lone in the mid - dle of the sea.

He sat high a - bove his bay, watch - ing all the cou - ples play and wish - ing that he had some - one, too. And from his

© 2014, 2015 Walt Disney Music Company and Pixar Talking Pictures
All Rights Reserved. Used by Permission.

Let It Go
from FROZEN

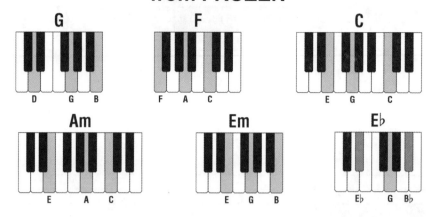

Music and Lyrics by Kristen Anderson-Lopez
and Robert Lopez

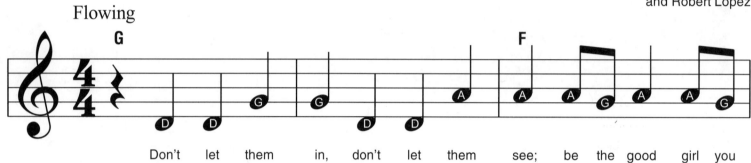

Don't let them in, don't let them see; be the good girl you

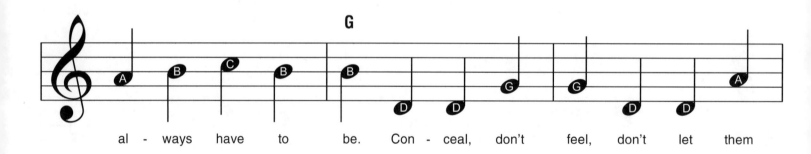

al - ways have to be. Con - ceal, don't feel, don't let them

know... _____ Well, now they know. _____

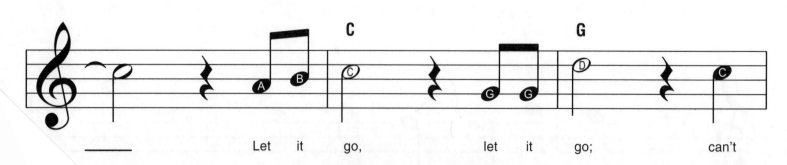

_____ Let it go, let it go; can't

© 2013 Wonderland Music Company, Inc.
All Rights Reserved. Used by Permission.

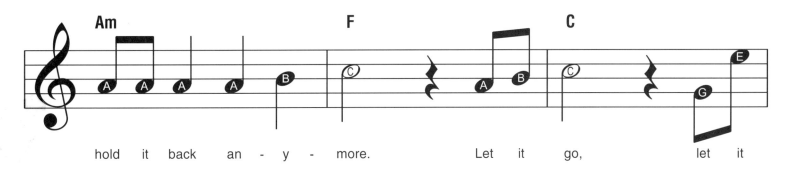

hold it back an - y - more. Let it go, let it

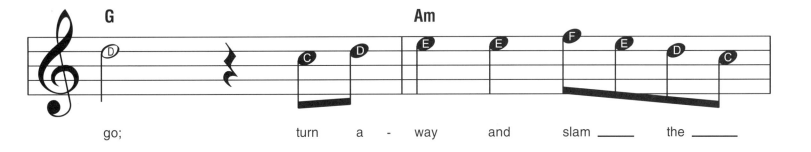

go; turn a - way and slam _____ the _____

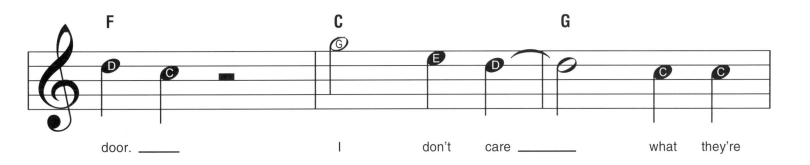

door. _____ I don't care _____ what they're

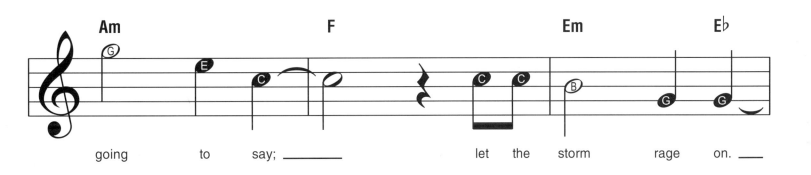

going to say; _____ let the storm rage on. _____

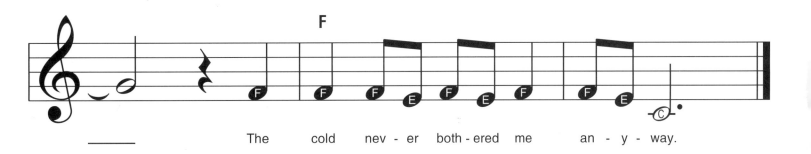

_____ The cold nev - er both - ered me an - y - way.

Let's Go Fly a Kite

from MARY POPPINS

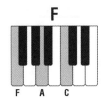
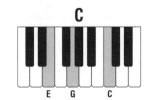

Words and Music by Richard M. Sherman
and Robert B. Sherman

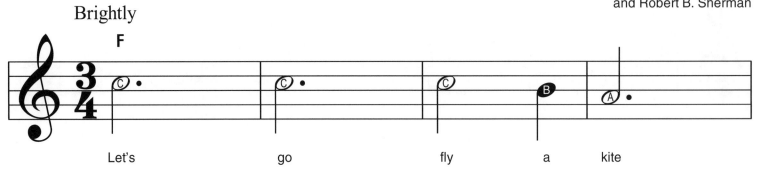

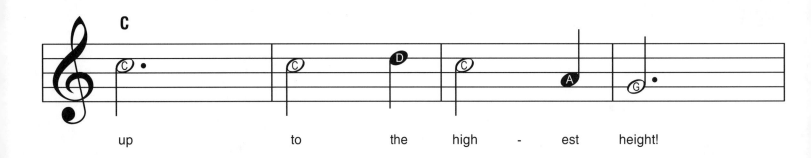

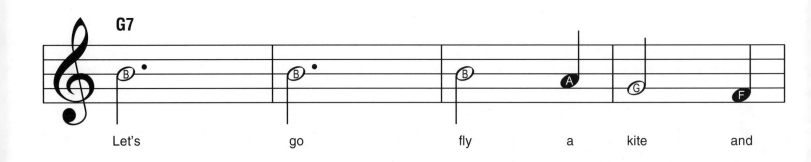

© 1963 Wonderland Music Company, Inc.
Copyright Renewed.
All Rights Reserved. Used by Permission.

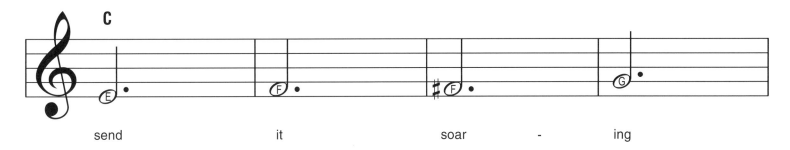

send   it   soar -   ing

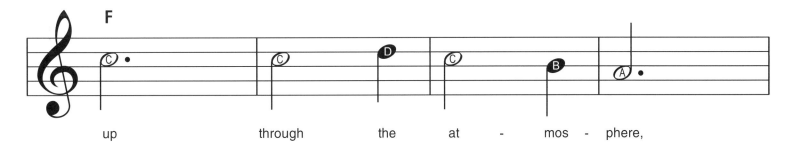

up   through   the   at - mos - phere,

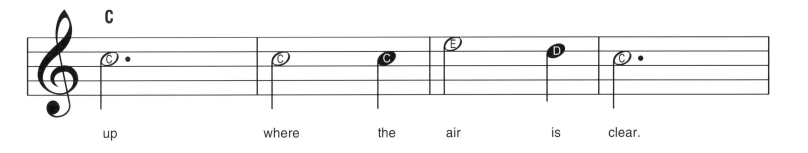

up   where   the   air   is   clear.

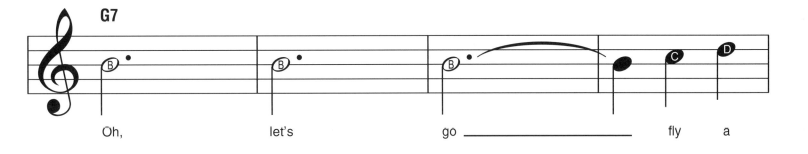

Oh,   let's   go _____ fly a

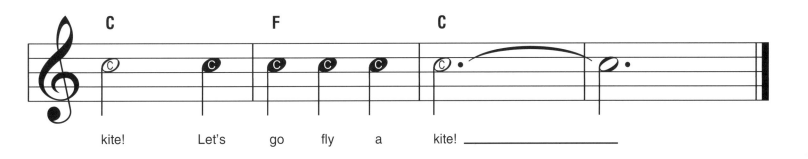

kite! Let's go fly a kite! _____

Mickey Mouse March
from Walt Disney's THE MICKEY MOUSE CLUB

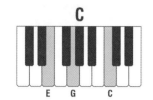
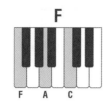

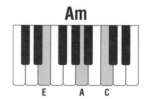
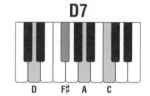

Words and Music by
Jimmie Dodd

Bright March

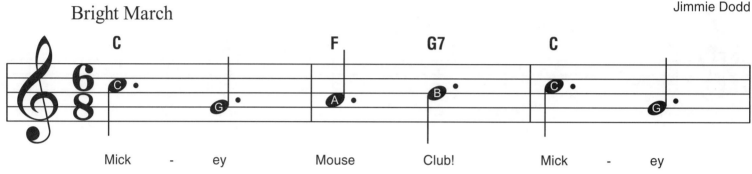

Mick - ey   Mouse   Club!   Mick - ey

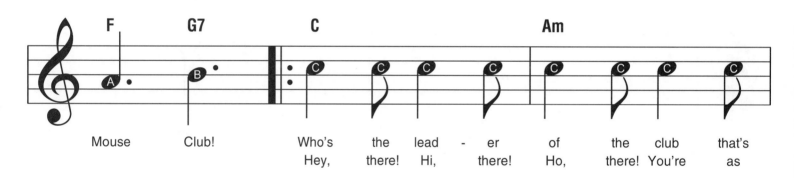

Mouse   Club!   Who's   the   lead - er   of   the   club   that's
                  Hey,   there! Hi,   there!   Ho,   there! You're   as

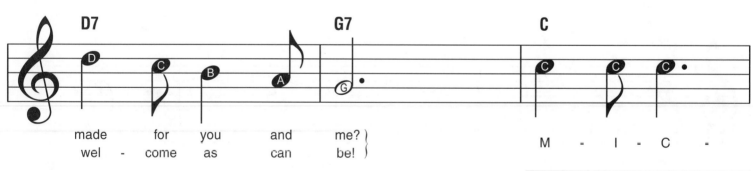

made   for   you   and   me?)
wel - come   as   can   be!)   M - I - C -

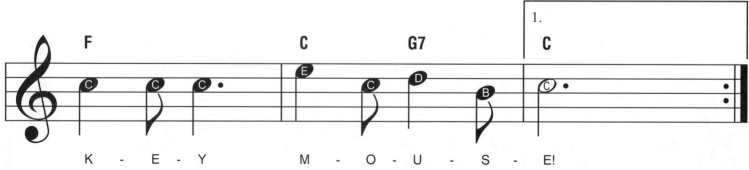

K - E - Y   M - O - U - S - E!

© 1955 Walt Disney Music Company
Copyright Renewed.
All Rights Reserved. Used by Permission.

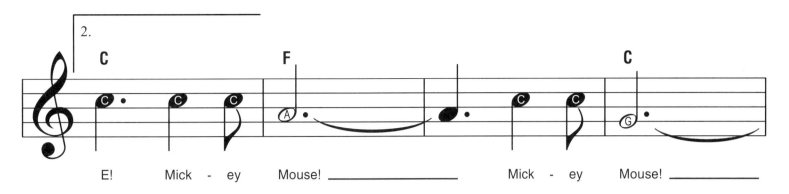

E! Mick - ey Mouse! _____ Mick - ey Mouse! _____

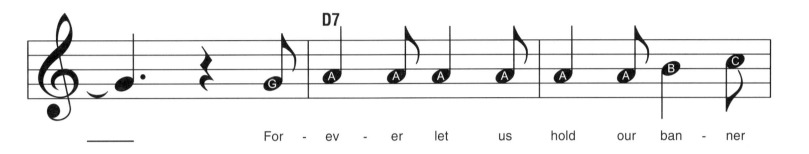

_____ For - ev - er let us hold our ban - ner

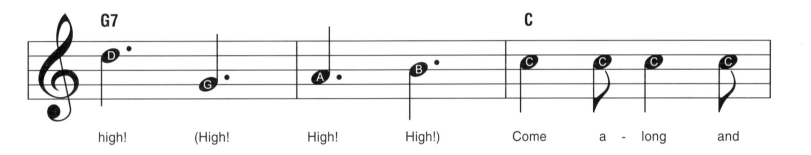

high! (High! High! High!) Come a - long and

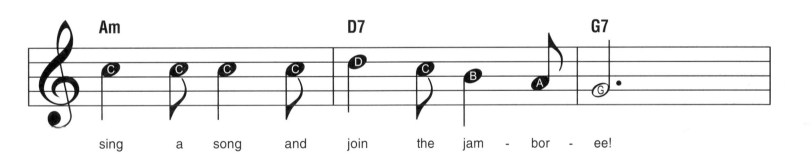

sing a song and join the jam - bor - ee!

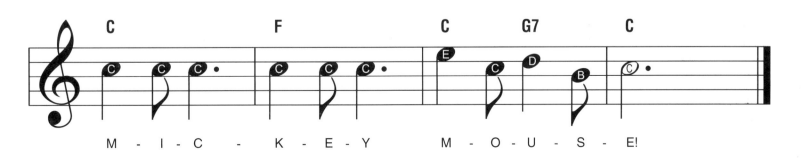

M - I - C - K - E - Y M - O - U - S - E!

My Funny Friend and Me

from THE EMPEROR'S NEW GROOVE

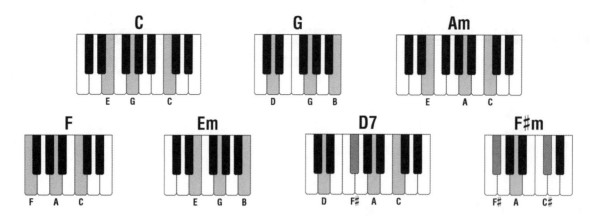

Lyrics by Sting
Music by Sting and David Hartley

Moderately slow

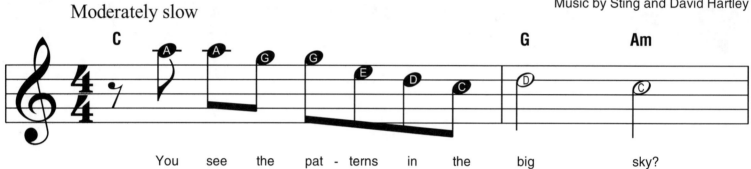

You see the pat - terns in the big sky?

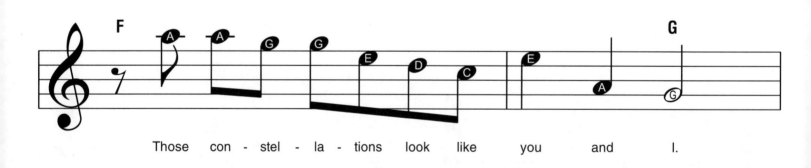

Those con - stel - la - tions look like you and I.

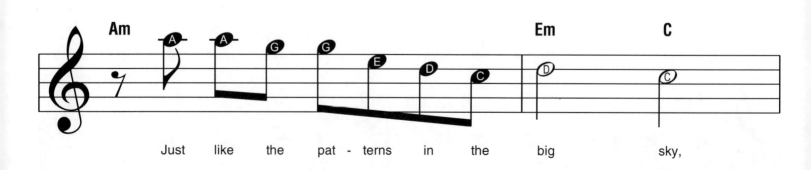

Just like the pat - terns in the big sky,

© 2000 Wonderland Music Company, Inc.
All Rights Reserved. Used by Permission.

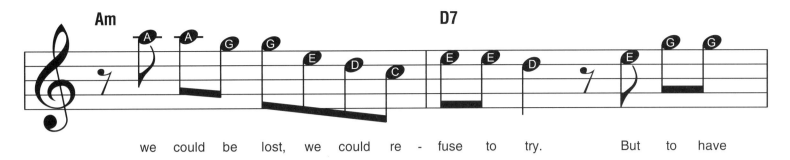

we could be lost, we could re - fuse to try. But to have

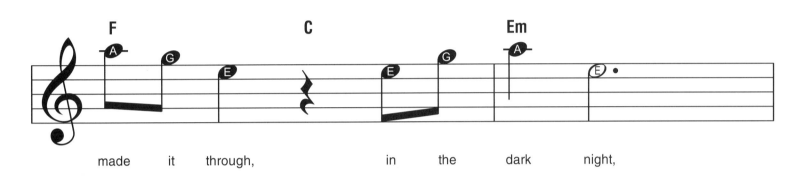

made it through, in the dark night,

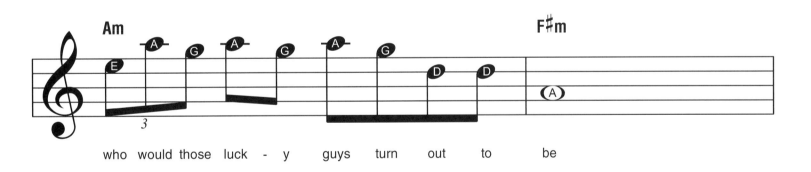

who would those luck - y guys turn out to be

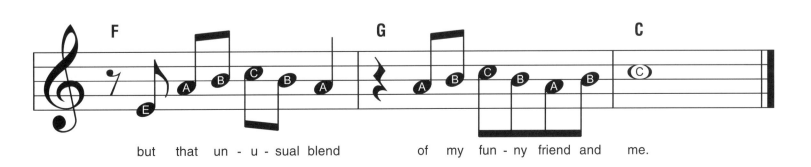

but that un - u - sual blend of my fun - ny friend and me.

Part of Your World
from THE LITTLE MERMAID

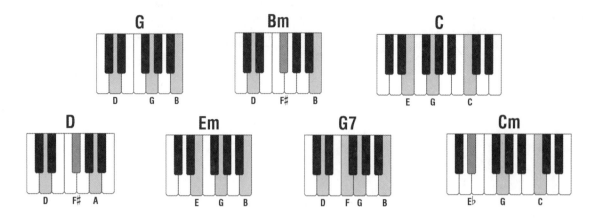

Music by Alan Menken
Lyrics by Howard Ashman

Moderately

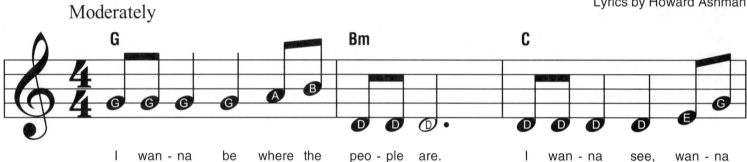

I wan - na be where the peo - ple are. I wan - na see, wan - na

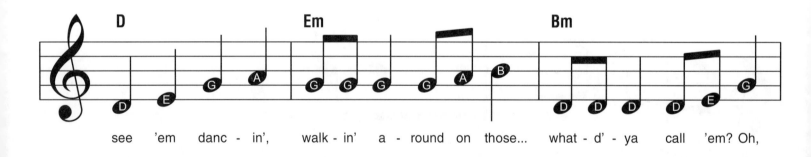

see 'em danc - in', walk - in' a - round on those... what - d' - ya call 'em? Oh,

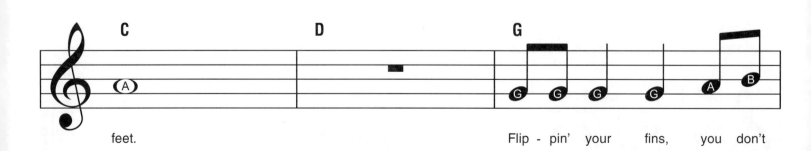

feet.   Flip - pin' your fins, you don't

© 1988 Wonderland Music Company, Inc. and Walt Disney Music Company
All Rights Reserved. Used by Permission.

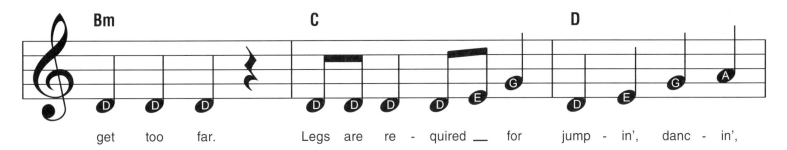

get too far. Legs are re - quired __ for jump - in', danc - in',

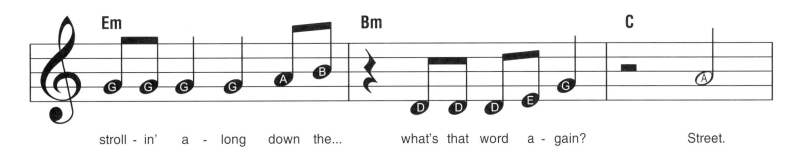

stroll - in' a - long down the... what's that word a - gain? Street.

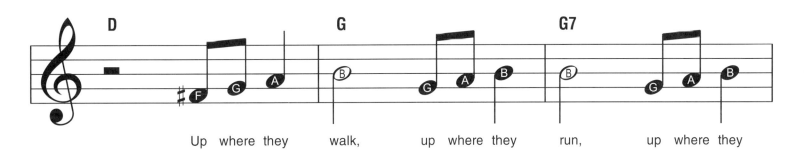

Up where they walk, up where they run, up where they

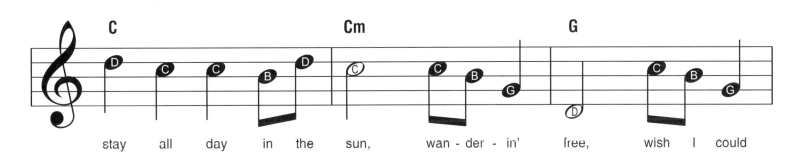

stay all day in the sun, wan - der - in' free, wish I could

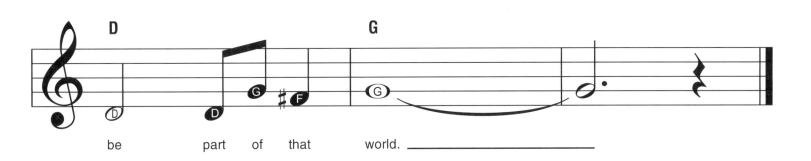

be part of that world. _____

Reflection

from MULAN

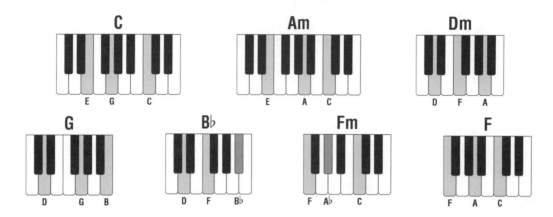

Music by Matthew Wilder
Lyrics by David Zippel

Moderately

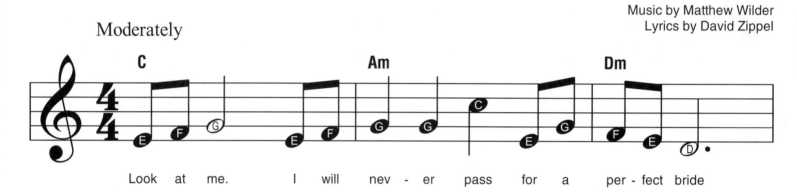

Look at me. I will nev - er pass for a per - fect bride

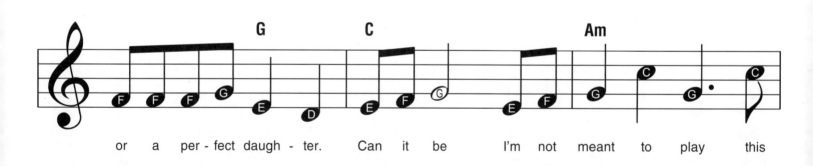

or a per - fect daugh - ter. Can it be I'm not meant to play this

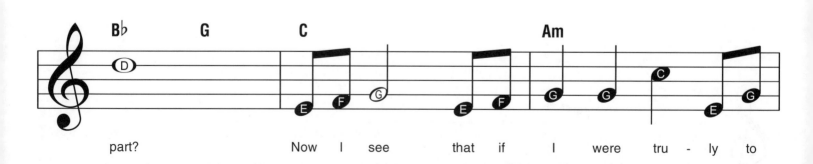

part? Now I see that if I were tru - ly to

© 1998 Walt Disney Music Company
All Rights Reserved. Used by Permission.

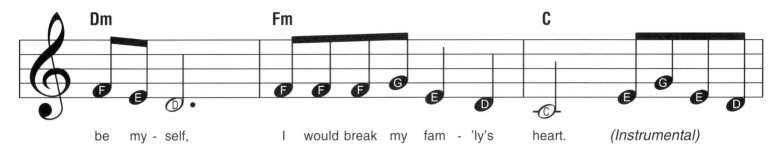

be my - self,   I would break my fam - 'ly's   heart.   *(Instrumental)*

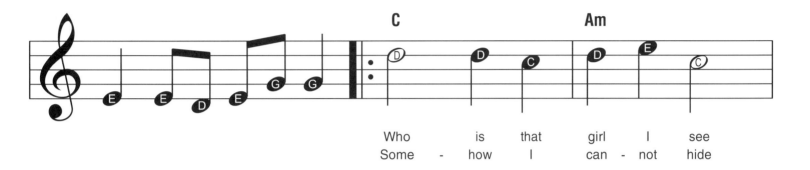

Who   is   that   girl   I   see
Some - how   I   can - not   hide

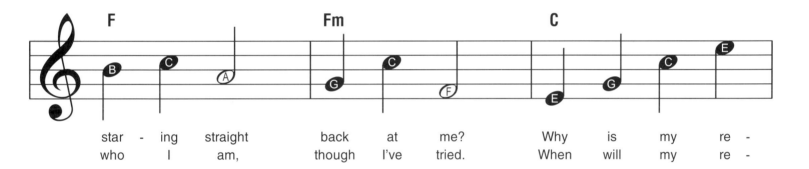

star - ing   straight   back   at   me?   Why   is   my   re -
who   I   am,   though   I've   tried.   When   will   my   re -

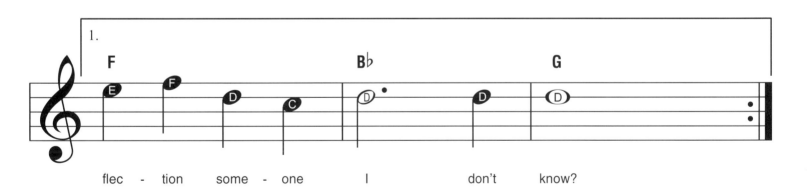

1.

flec - tion   some - one   I   don't   know?

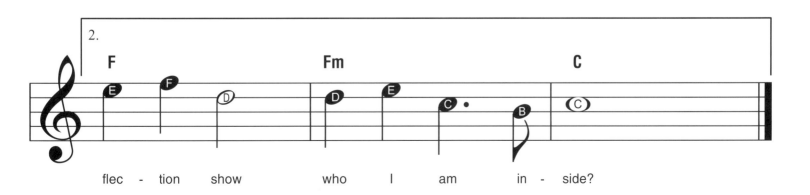

2.

flec - tion   show   who   I   am   in - side?

The Siamese Cat Song

from LADY AND THE TRAMP

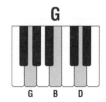
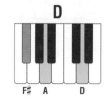

Words and Music by Peggy Lee
and Sonny Burke

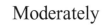

Moderately

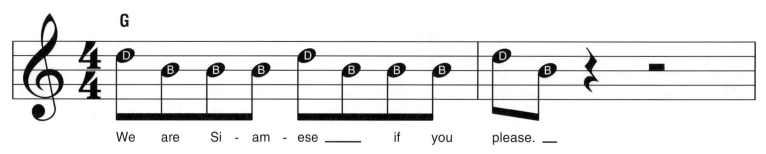

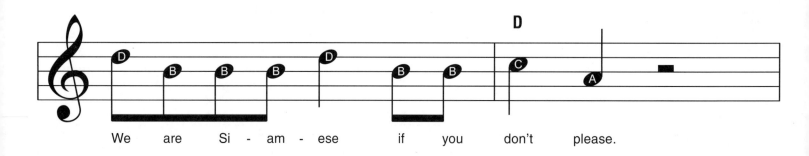

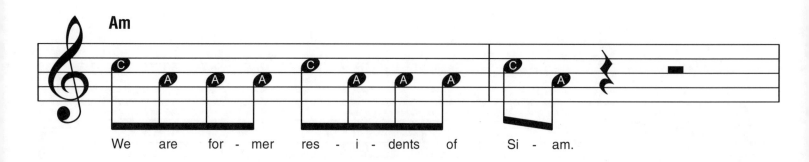

© 1953 Walt Disney Music Company
Copyright Renewed.
All Rights Reserved. Used by Permission.

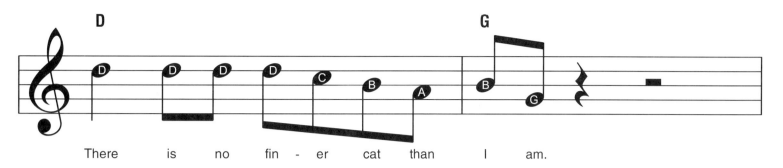

There is no fin - er cat than I am.

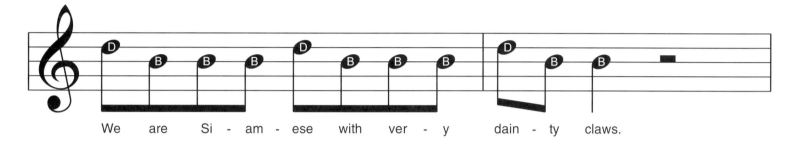

We are Si - am - ese with ver - y dain - ty claws.

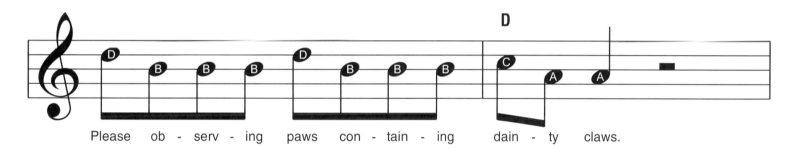

Please ob - serv - ing paws con - tain - ing dain - ty claws.

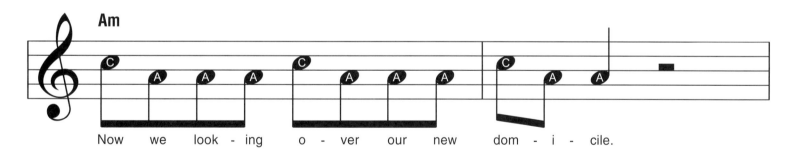

Now we look - ing o - ver our new dom - i - cile.

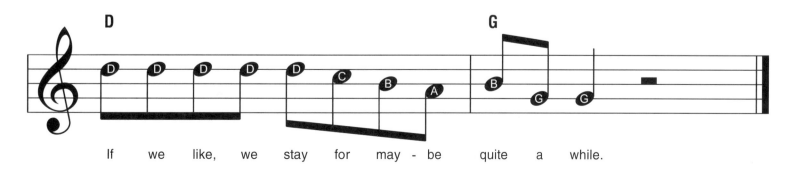

If we like, we stay for may - be quite a while.

Some Day My Prince Will Come

from SNOW WHITE AND THE SEVEN DWARFS

Words by Larry Morey
Music by Frank Churchill

Copyright © 1937 by Bourne Co. (ASCAP)
Copyright Renewed.
International Copyright Secured.   All Rights Reserved.

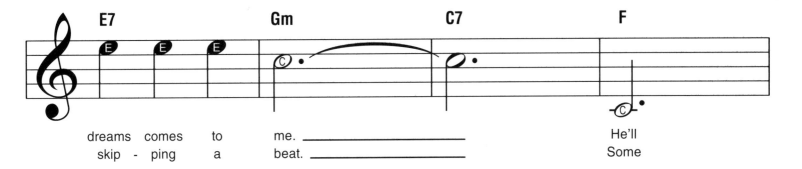

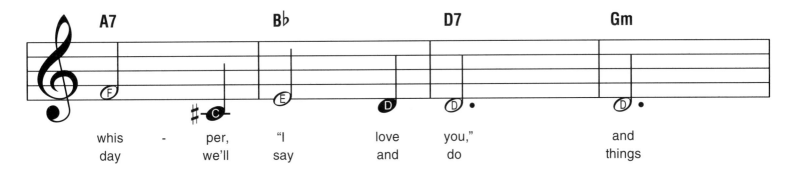

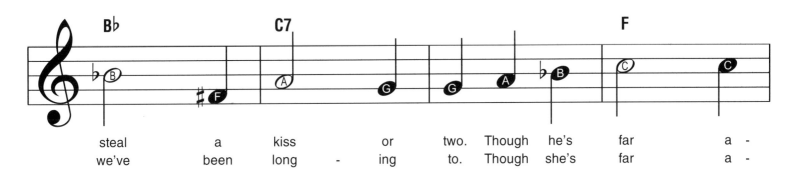

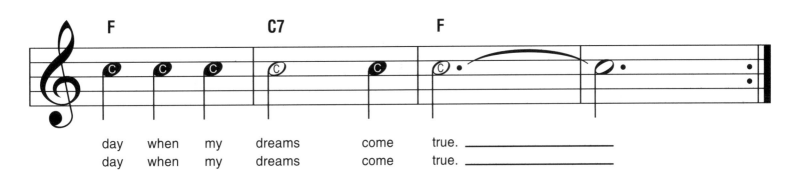

Someday

from THE HUNCHBACK OF NOTRE DAME

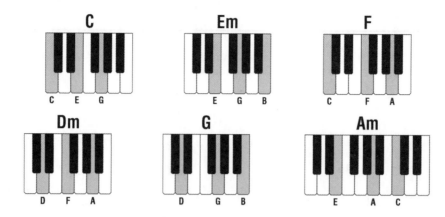

Music by Alan Menken
Lyrics by Stephen Schwartz

Moderately

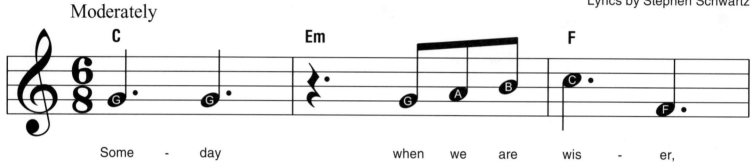

Some - day   when we are wis - er,

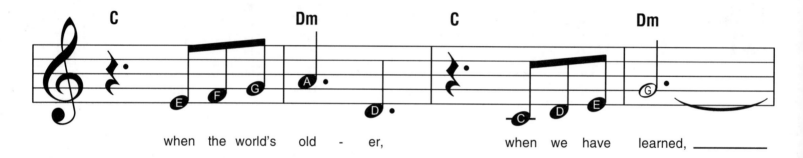

when the world's old - er,   when we have learned, _____

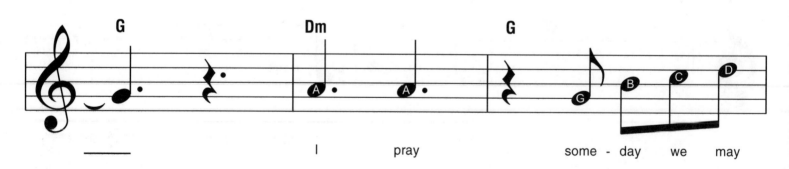

_____   I   pray   some - day we may

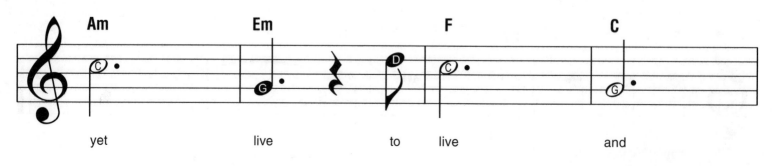

yet   live   to   live   and

© 1996 Wonderland Music Company, Inc. and Walt Disney Music Company
All Rights Reserved. Used by Permission.

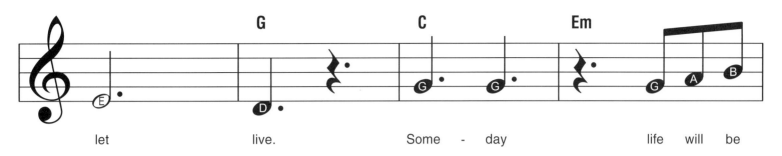

let   live.   Some - day   life will be

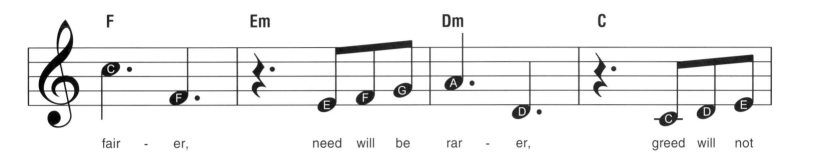

fair - er,   need will be rar - er,   greed will not

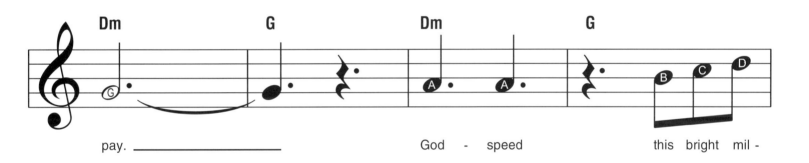

pay. _____   God - speed   this bright mil -

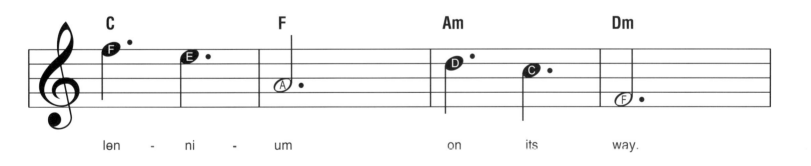

len - ni - um   on its way.

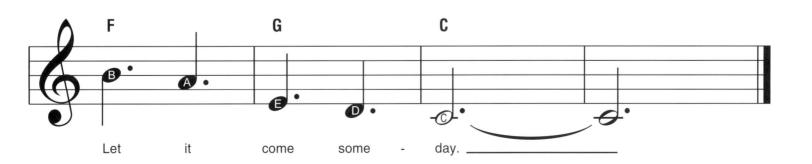

Let it come some - day. _____

A Spoonful of Sugar

from MARY POPPINS

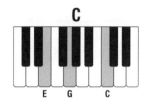 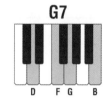 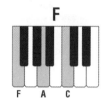 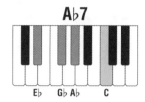 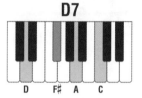

Words and Music by Richard M. Sherman
and Robert B. Sherman

Moderately fast

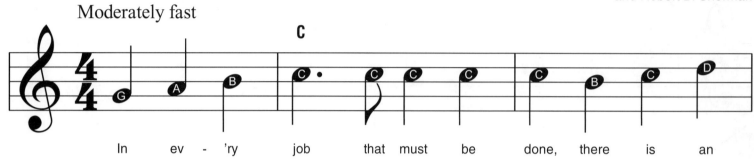

In ev - 'ry job that must be done, there is an

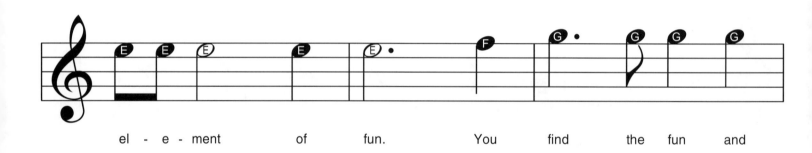

el - e - ment of fun. You find the fun and

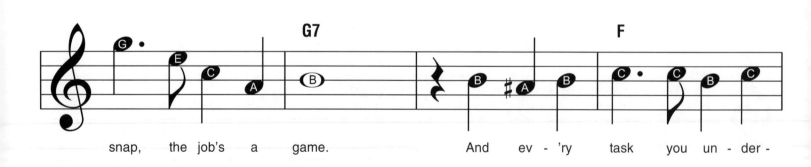

snap, the job's a game. And ev - 'ry task you un - der -

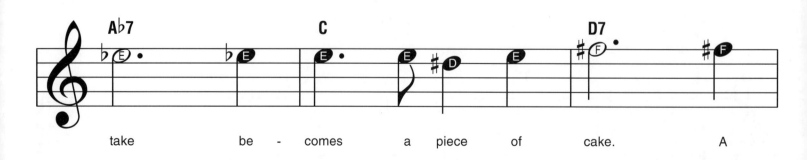

take be - comes a piece of cake. A

© 1963 Wonderland Music Company, Inc.
Copyright Renewed.
All Rights Reserved. Used by Permission.

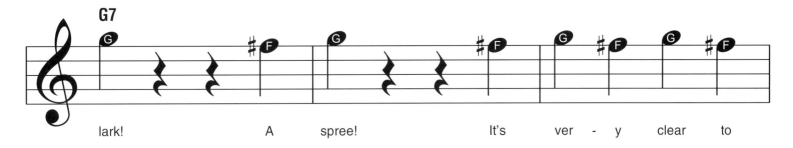

lark! A spree! It's ver - y clear to

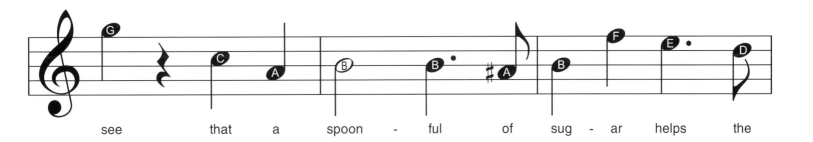

see that a spoon - ful of sug - ar helps the

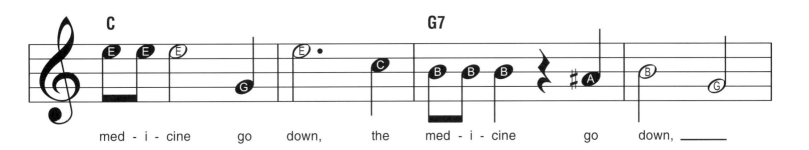

med - i - cine go down, the med - i - cine go down, _____

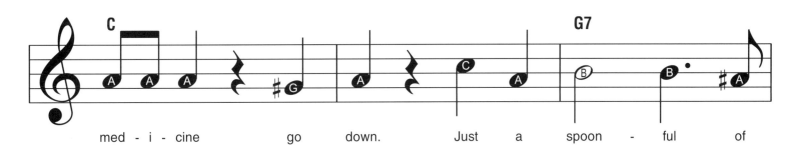

med - i - cine go down. Just a spoon - ful of

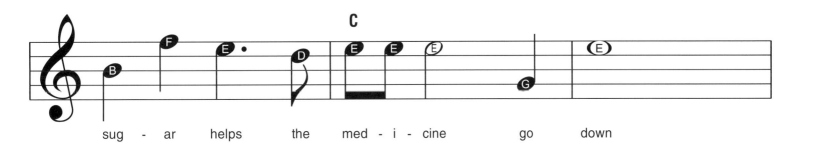

sug - ar helps the med - i - cine go down

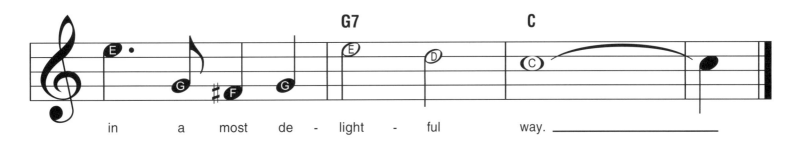

in a most de - light - ful way. _____

Supercalifragilisticexpialidocious

from MARY POPPINS

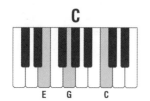 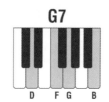 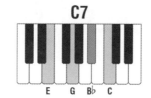 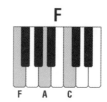 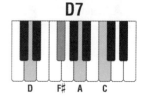

Words and Music by Richard M. Sherman
and Robert B. Sherman

Moderately fast

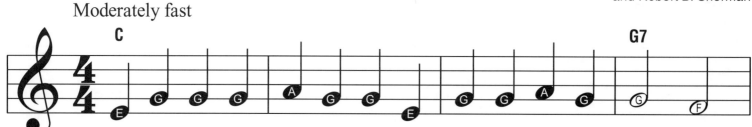

Su - per - cal - i - frag - il - is - tic - ex - pi - al - i - do - cious!

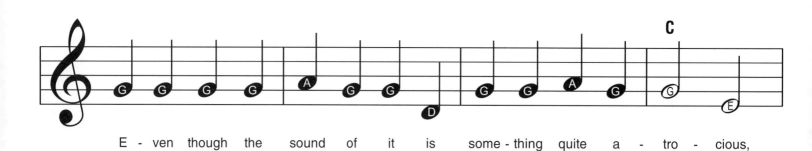

E - ven though the sound of it is some - thing quite a - tro - cious,

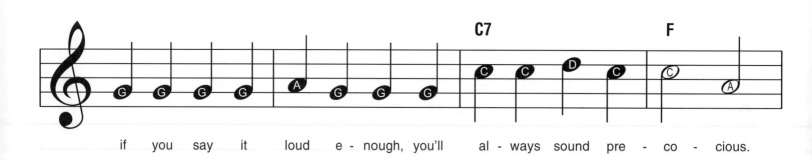

if you say it loud e - nough, you'll al - ways sound pre - co - cious.

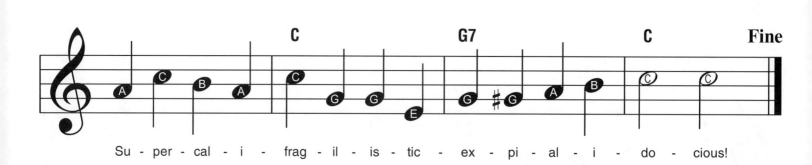

Su - per - cal - i - frag - il - is - tic - ex - pi - al - i - do - cious!

© 1963 Wonderland Music Company, Inc.
Copyright Renewed.
All Rights Reserved. Used by Permission.

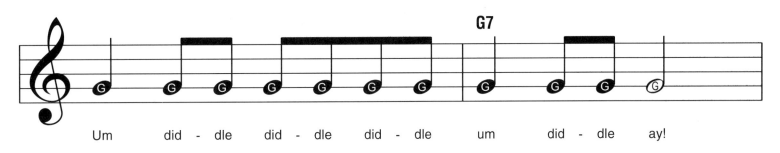

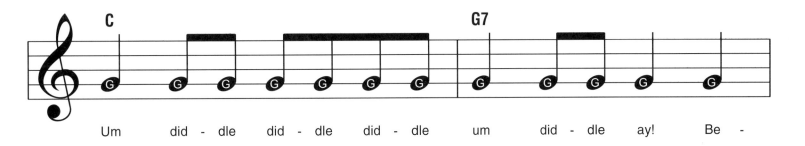

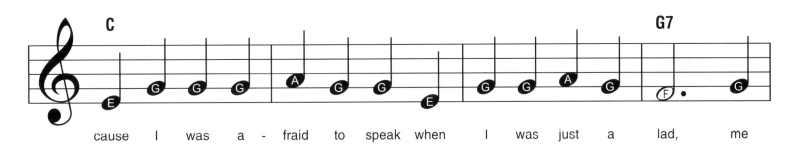

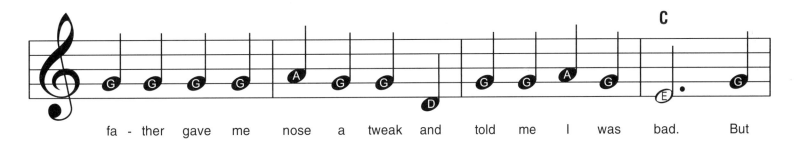

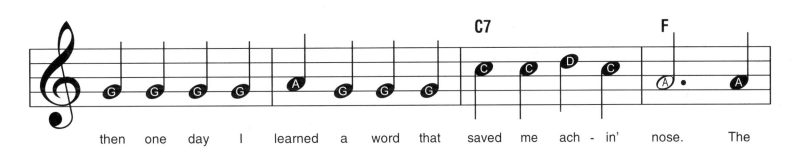

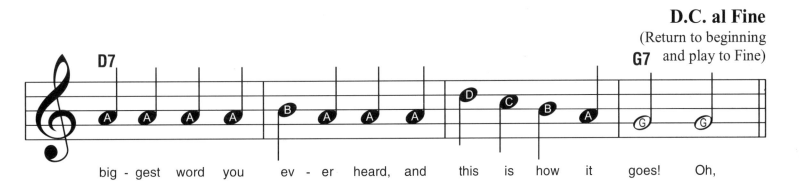

That's How You Know
from ENCHANTED

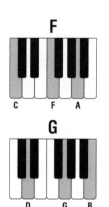
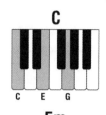
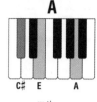
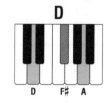
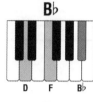
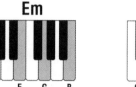

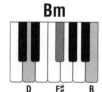

Music by Alan Menken
Lyrics by Stephen Schwartz

Moderately bright

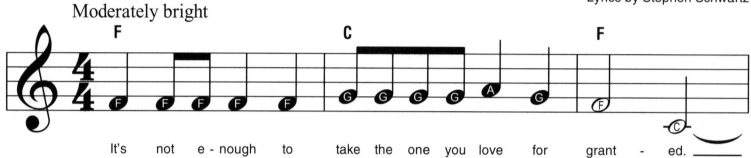

It's not e - nough to take the one you love for grant - ed. _____

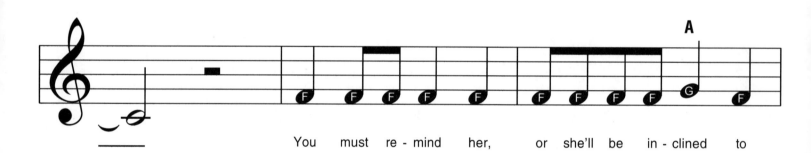

_____ You must re - mind her, or she'll be in - clined to

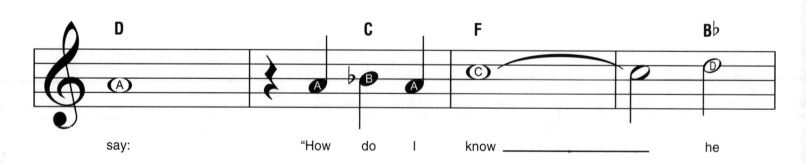

say: "How do I know _____ he

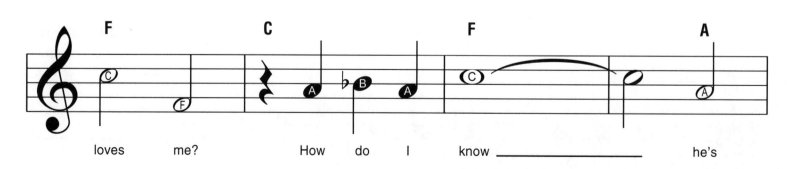

loves me? How do I know _____ he's

© 2007 Wonderland Music Company, Inc. and Walt Disney Music Company
All Rights Reserved. Used by Permission.

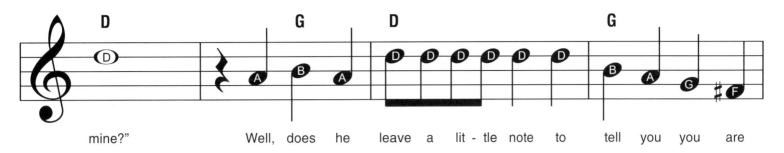

mine?" Well, does he leave a lit-tle note to tell you you are

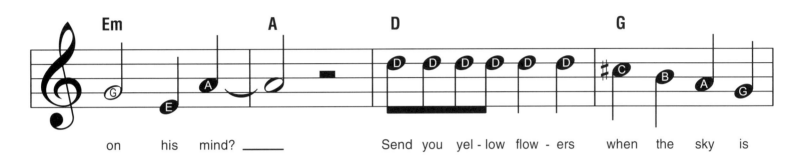

on his mind? _____ Send you yel-low flow-ers when the sky is

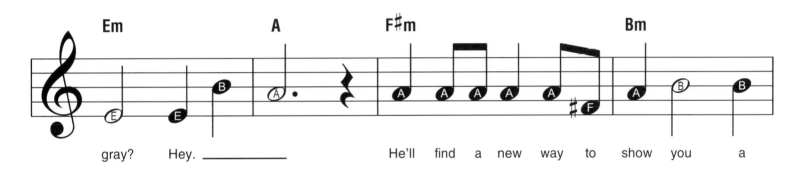

gray? Hey. _____ He'll find a new way to show you a

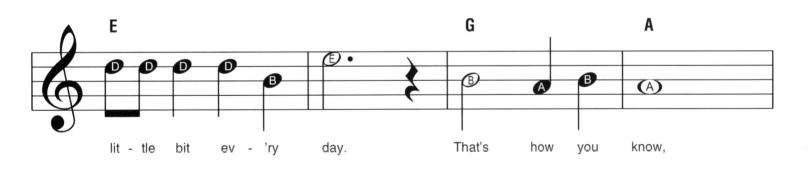

lit-tle bit ev-'ry day. That's how you know,

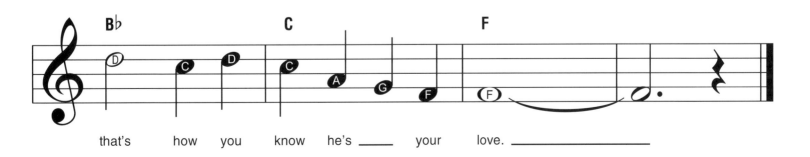

that's how you know he's _____ your love. _____

True Love's Kiss

from ENCHANTED

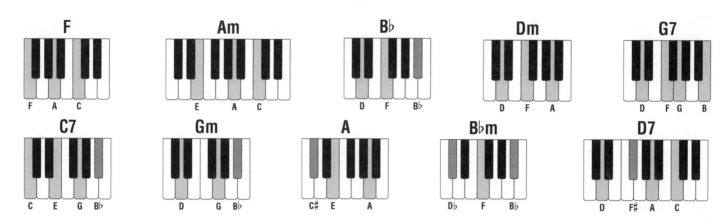

Music by Alan Menken
Lyrics by Stephen Schwartz

Moderately

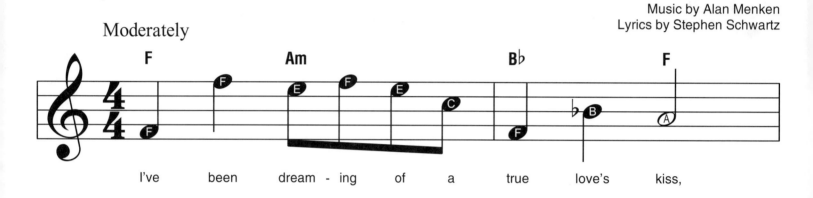

I've been dream-ing of a true love's kiss,

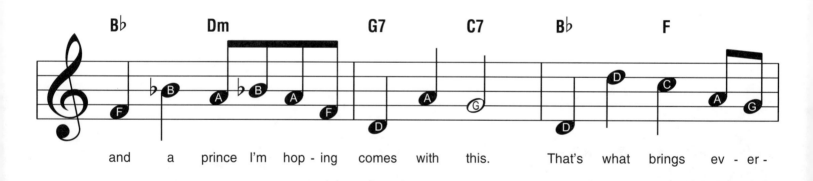

and a prince I'm hop-ing comes with this. That's what brings ev-er-

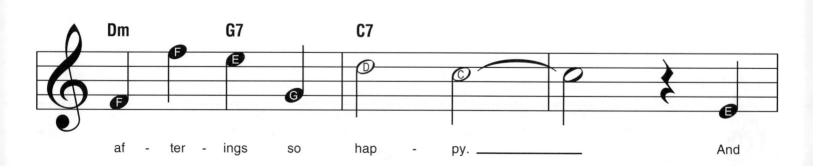

af-ter-ings so hap-py. _____ And

© 2007 Wonderland Music Company, Inc. and Walt Disney Music Company
All Rights Reserved. Used by Permission.

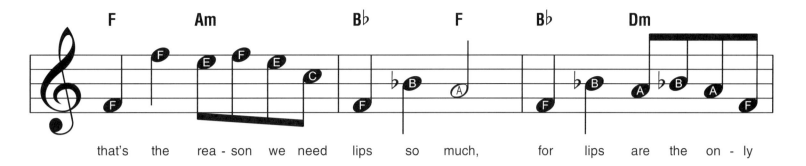

that's the rea - son we need lips so much, for lips are the on - ly

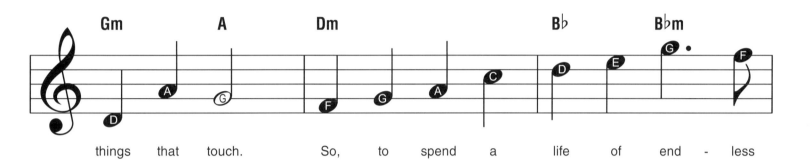

things that touch. So, to spend a life of end - less

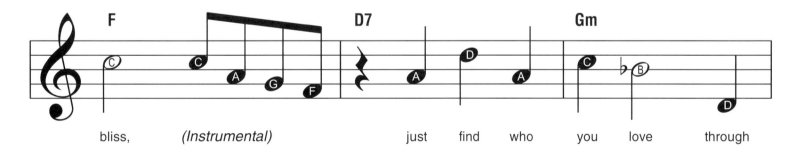

bliss, *(Instrumental)* just find who you love through

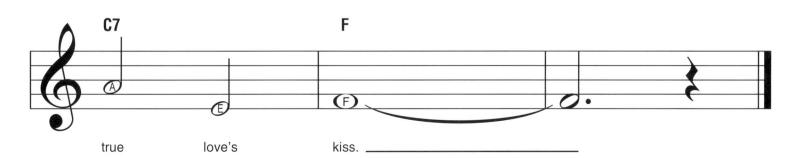

true love's kiss. _____

The Unbirthday Song
from ALICE IN WONDERLAND

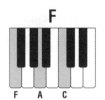 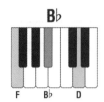 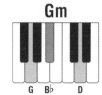 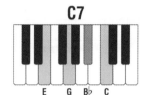 

Words and Music by Mack David,
Al Hoffman and Jerry Livingston

Moderately fast

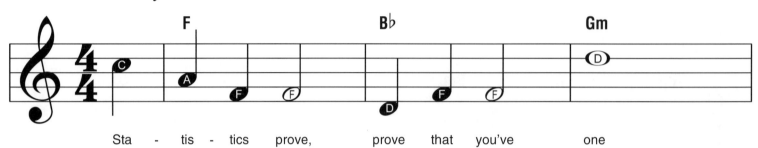

Sta - tis - tics prove, prove that you've one

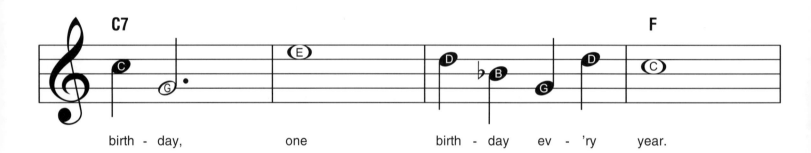

birth - day, one birth - day ev - 'ry year.

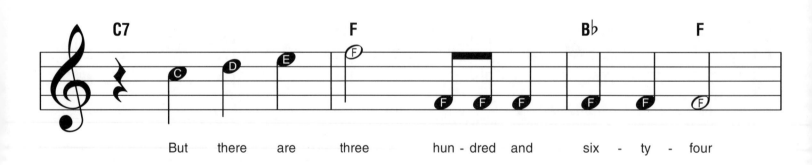

But there are three hun - dred and six - ty - four

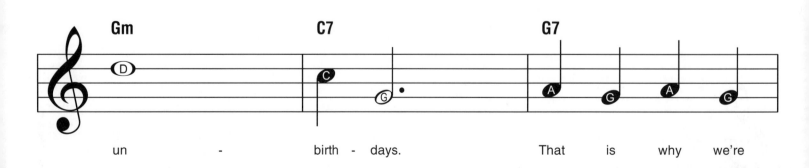

un - birth - days. That is why we're

© 1948 Walt Disney Music Company
Copyright Renewed.
All Rights Reserved. Used by Permission.

gath - ered here to cheer. _____ A

ver - y mer - ry un - birth - day to you, to

you. A ver - y mer - ry un - birth - day to

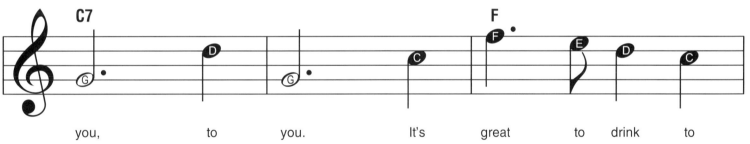

you, to you. It's great to drink to

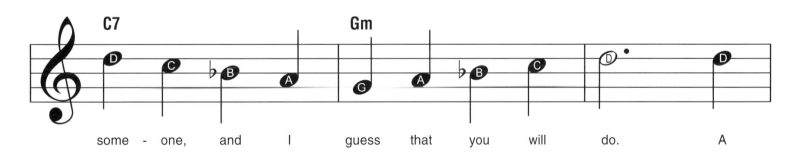

some - one, and I guess that you will do. A

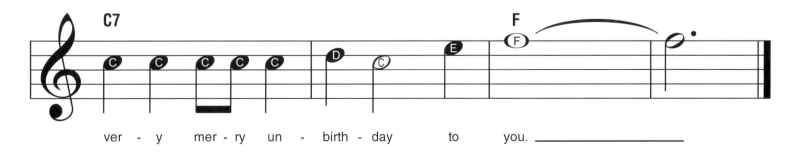

ver - y mer - ry un - birth - day to you. _____

Under the Sea
from THE LITTLE MERMAID

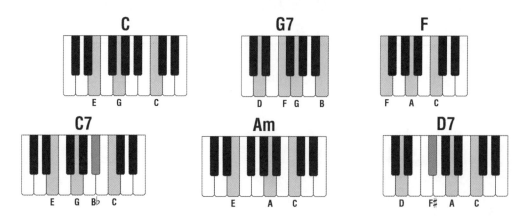

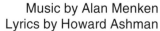

Music by Alan Menken
Lyrics by Howard Ashman

Brightly

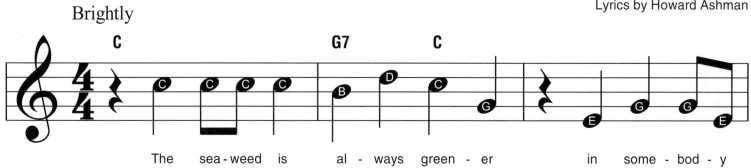

The sea-weed is al - ways green - er in some - bod - y

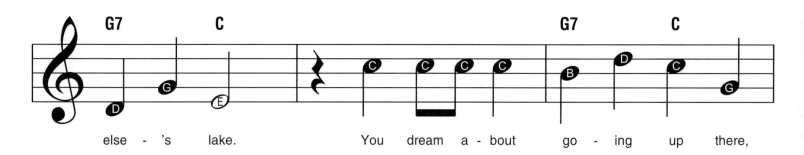

else - 's lake. You dream a - bout go - ing up there,

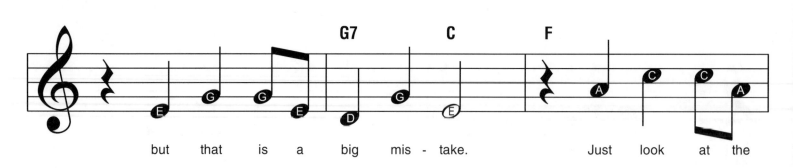

but that is a big mis - take. Just look at the

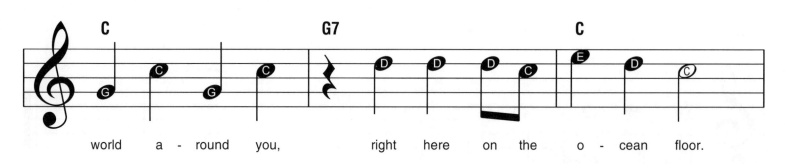

world a - round you, right here on the o - cean floor.

© 1988 Wonderland Music Company, Inc. and Walt Disney Music Company
All Rights Reserved. Used by Permission.

A Whale of a Tale
from 20,000 LEAGUES UNDER THE SEA

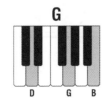
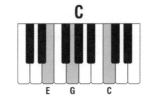
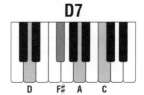

Words and Music by Norman Gimbel
and Al Hoffman

Moderately fast

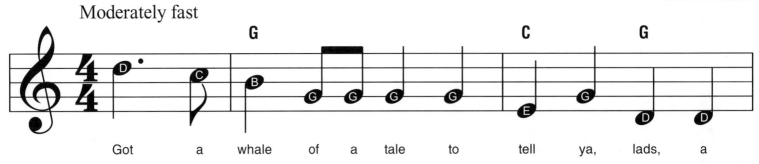

Got a whale of a tale to tell ya, lads, a

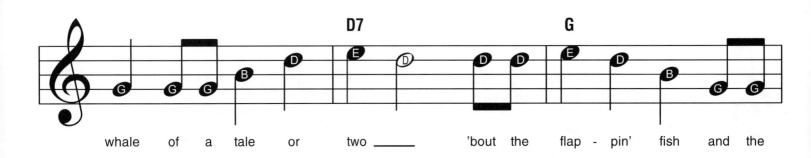

whale of a tale or two ____ 'bout the flap-pin' fish and the

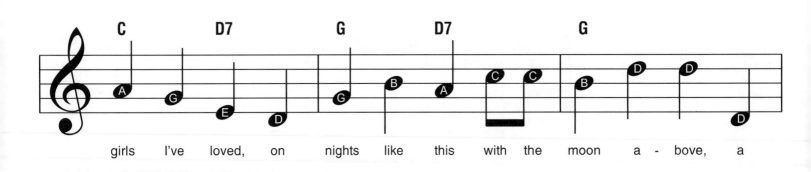

girls I've loved, on nights like this with the moon a - bove, a

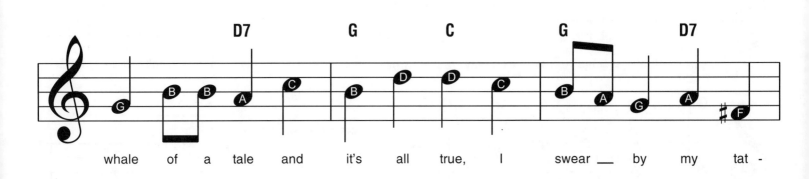

whale of a tale and it's all true, I swear ____ by my tat -

© 1953 Wonderland Music Company, Inc.
Copyright Renewed.
All Rights Reserved. Used by Permission.

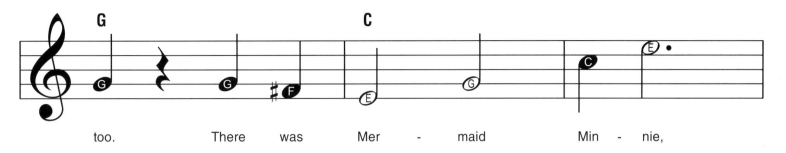

too. There was Mer - maid Min - nie,

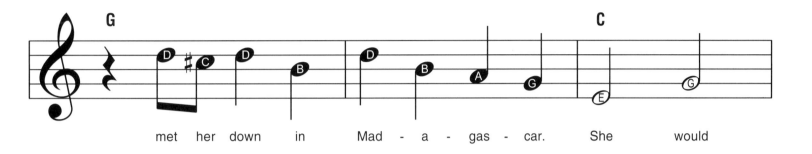

met her down in Mad - a - gas - car. She would

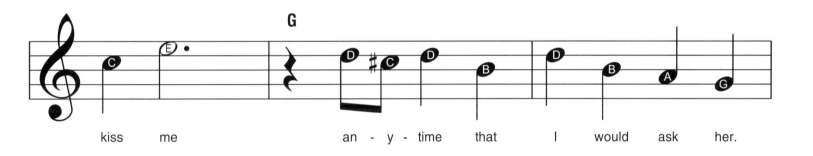

kiss me an - y - time that I would ask her.

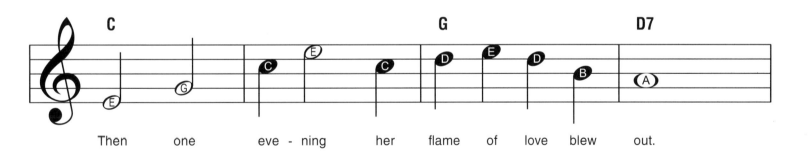

Then one eve - ning her flame of love blew out.

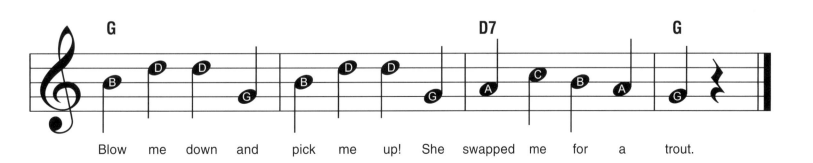

Blow me down and pick me up! She swapped me for a trout.

When She Loved Me

from TOY STORY 2

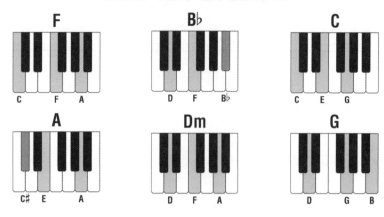

Music and Lyrics by
Randy Newman

Tenderly

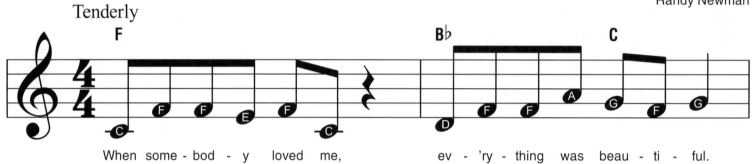

When some-bod-y loved me, ev-'ry-thing was beau-ti-ful.

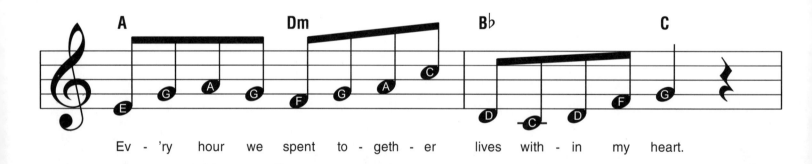

Ev-'ry hour we spent to-geth-er lives with-in my heart.

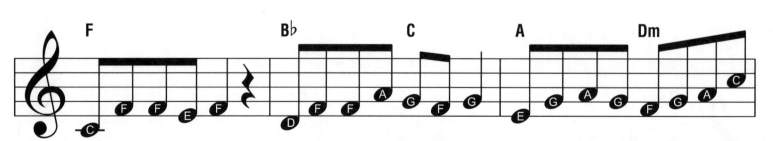

And when she was sad, I was there to dry her tears. And when she was hap-py, so was

© 1999 Walt Disney Music Company and Pixar Talking Pictures
All Rights Reserved. Used by Permission.

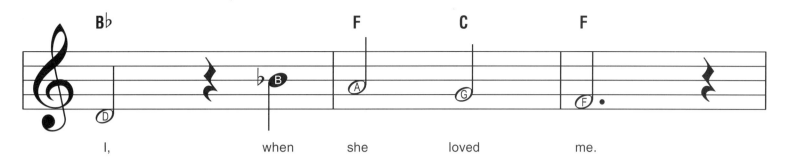

I,   when   she   loved   me.

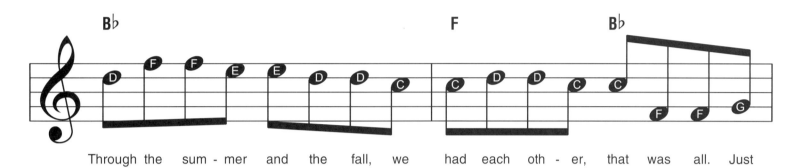

Through the sum - mer and the fall, we had each oth - er, that was all. Just

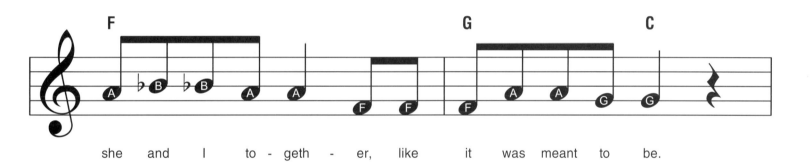

she and I to - geth - er, like it was meant to be.

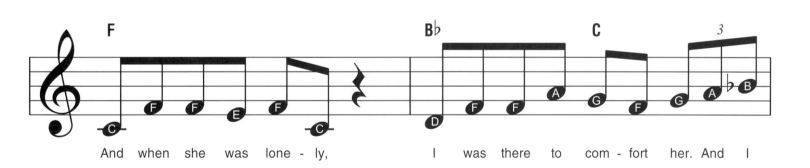

And when she was lone - ly,   I was there to com - fort her. And I

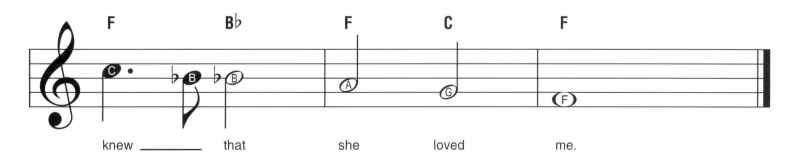

knew _____ that   she   loved   me.

When You Wish Upon a Star
from PINOCCHIO

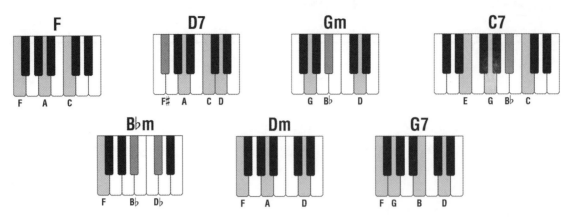

Words by Ned Washington
Music by Leigh Harline

Moderately

When   you   wish   up - on   a   star,   makes   no   dif - f'rence
If   your   heart   is   in   your   dream,   no   re - quest   is

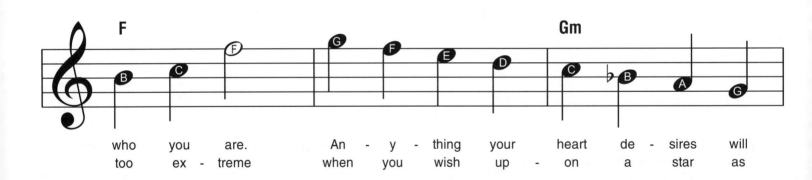

who   you   are.   An - y - thing   your   heart   de - sires   will
too   ex - treme   when   you   wish   up - on   a   star   as

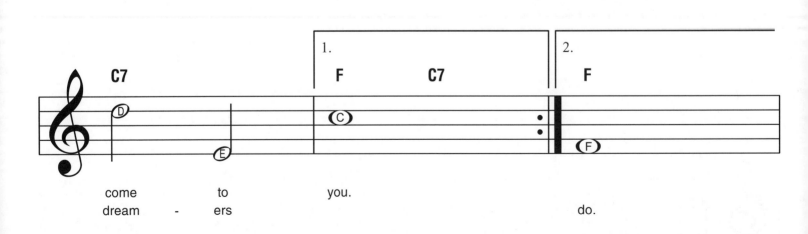

come   to   you.
dream - ers   do.

Copyright © 1940 by Bourne Co. (ASCAP)
Copyright Renewed.
International Copyright Secured.   All Rights Reserved.

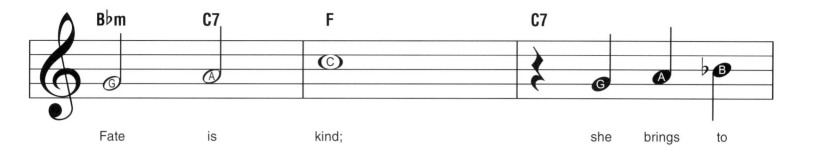

Fate   is   kind;   she   brings   to

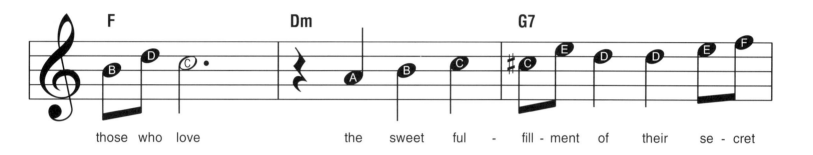

those who love   the   sweet   ful - fill - ment of   their   se - cret

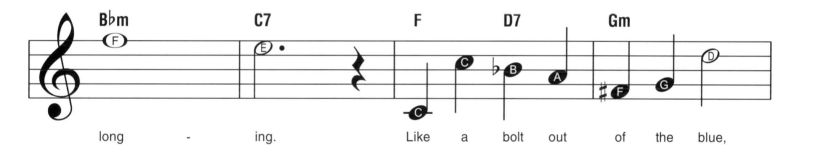

long   -   ing.   Like   a   bolt   out   of   the   blue,

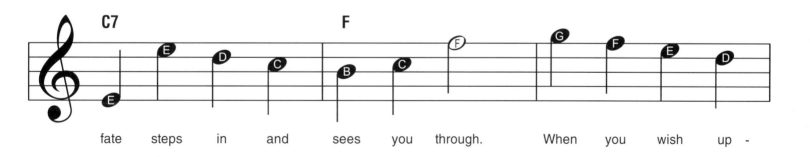

fate   steps   in   and   sees   you   through.   When   you   wish   up -

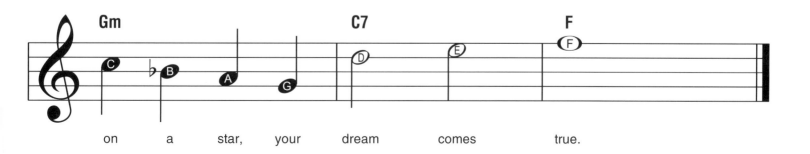

on   a   star,   your   dream   comes   true.

Whistle While You Work

from SNOW WHITE AND THE SEVEN DWARFS

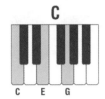
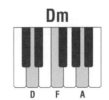
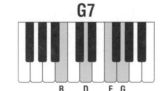
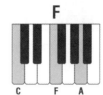
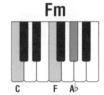

Words by Larry Morey
Music by Frank Churchill

Cheerfully

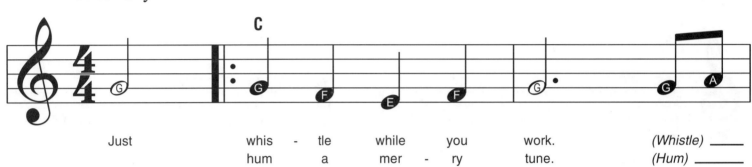

Just whis - tle while you work. *(Whistle)* ____
hum a mer - ry tune. *(Hum)* ____

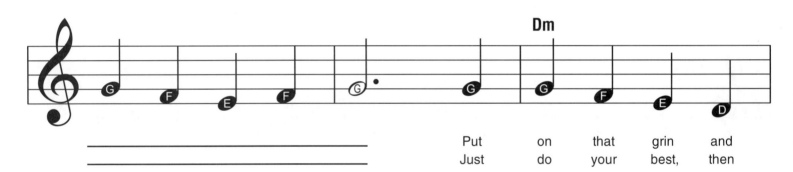

Put on that grin and
Just do your best, and then

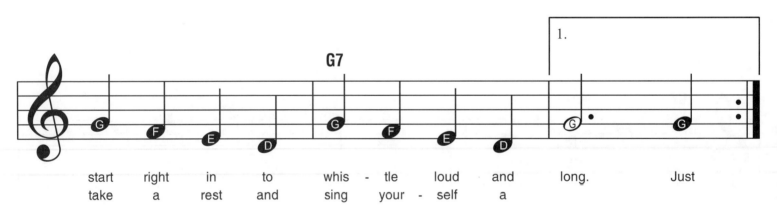

start right in to whis - tle loud and long. Just
take a rest and sing your - self a

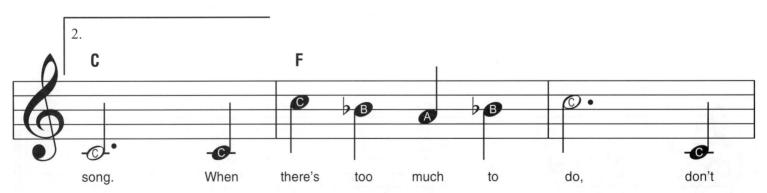

song. When there's too much to do, don't

Copyright © 1937 by Bourne Co. (ASCAP)
Copyright Renewed.
International Copyright Secured.   All Rights Reserved.

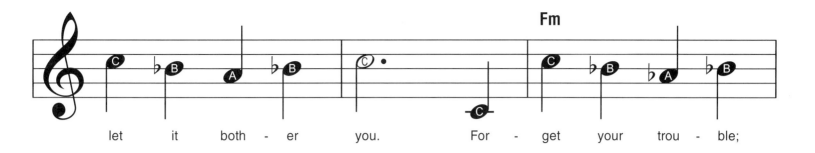

let it both - er you. For - get your trou - ble;

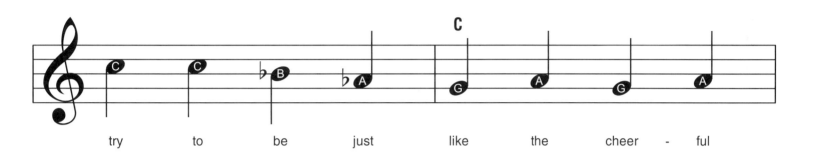

try to be just like the cheer - ful

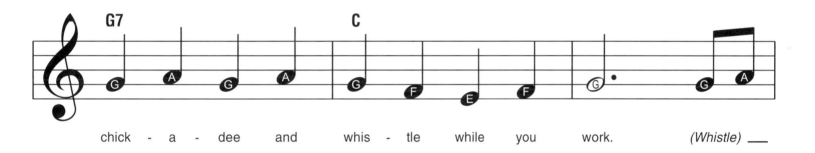

chick - a - dee and whis - tle while you work. *(Whistle)* __

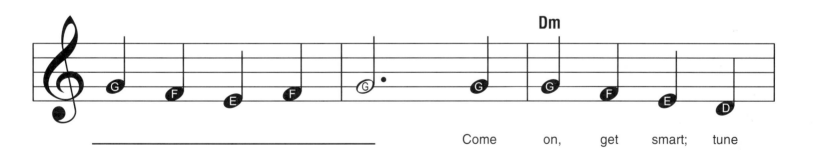

Come on, get smart; tune

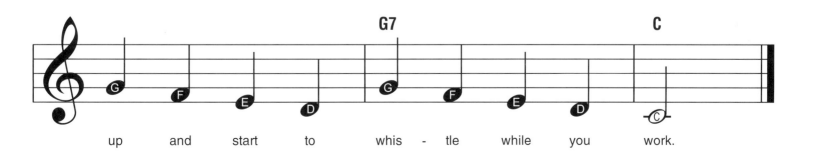

up and start to whis - tle while you work.

Who's Afraid of the Big Bad Wolf?

from THREE LITTLE PIGS

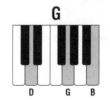
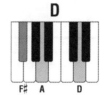

Words and Music by Frank Churchill
Additional Lyric by Ann Ronell

Brightly

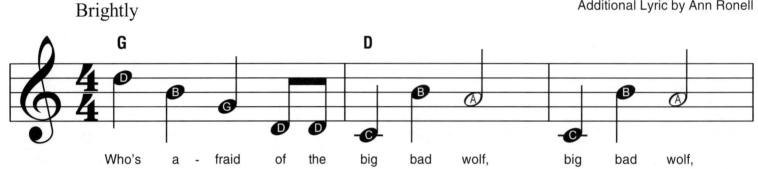

Who's a - fraid of the big bad wolf, big bad wolf,

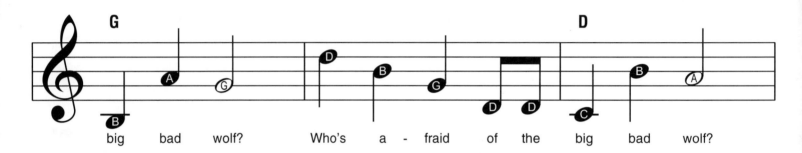

big bad wolf? Who's a - fraid of the big bad wolf?

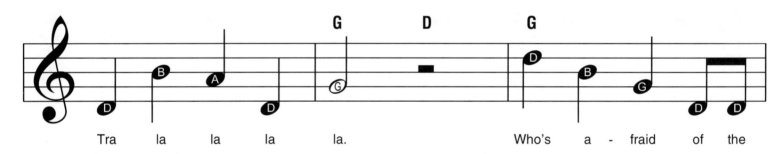

Tra la la la la. Who's a - fraid of the

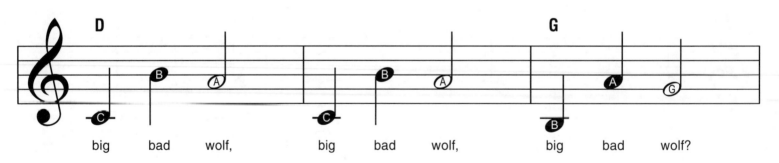

big bad wolf, big bad wolf, big bad wolf?

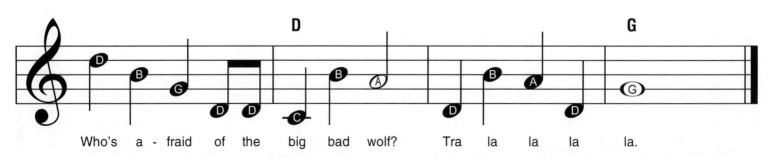

Who's a - fraid of the big bad wolf? Tra la la la la.

Copyright © 1933 by Bourne Co. (ASCAP)
Copyright Renewed.
International Copyright Secured.   All Rights Reserved.

Written in the Stars
from AIDA

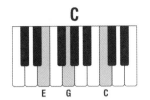 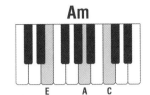 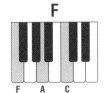 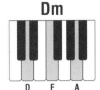 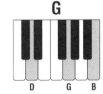

Music by Elton John
Lyrics by Tim Rice

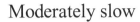

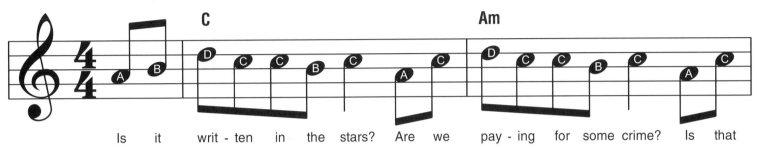

Is it writ-ten in the stars? Are we pay-ing for some crime? Is that

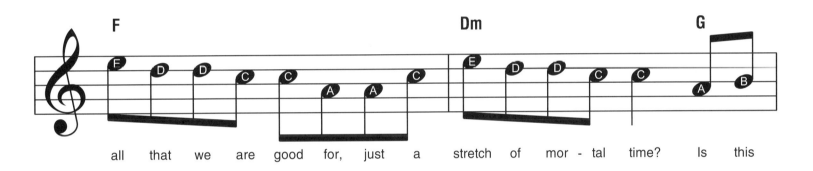

all that we are good for, just a stretch of mor-tal time? Is this

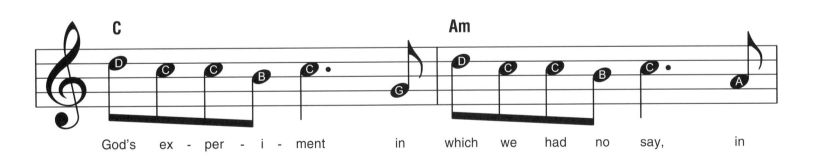

God's ex-per-i-ment in which we had no say, in

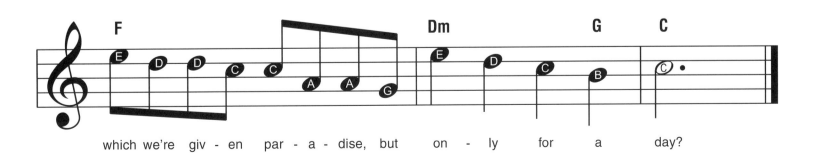

which we're giv-en par-a-dise, but on-ly for a day?

© 1999 Wonderland Music Company, Inc., Happenstance Ltd. and Evadon Ltd.
All Rights Reserved. Used by Permission.

A Whole New World
from ALADDIN

Music by Alan Menken
Lyrics by Tim Rice

© 1992 Wonderland Music Company, Inc. and Walt Disney Music Company
All Rights Reserved. Used by Permission.

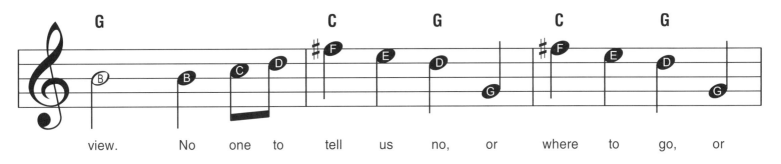

view. No one to tell us no, or where to go, or

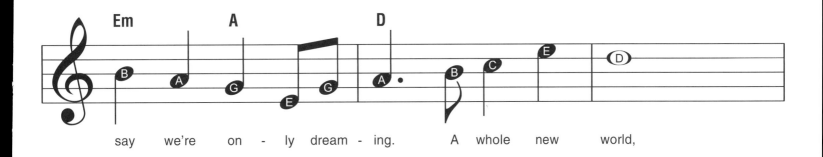

say we're on - ly dream - ing. A whole new world,

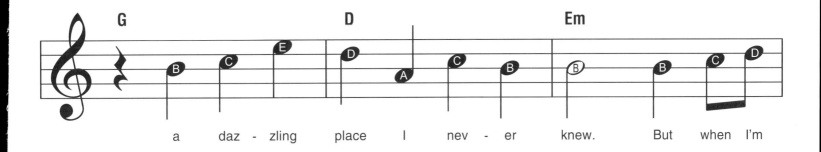

a daz - zling place I nev - er knew. But when I'm

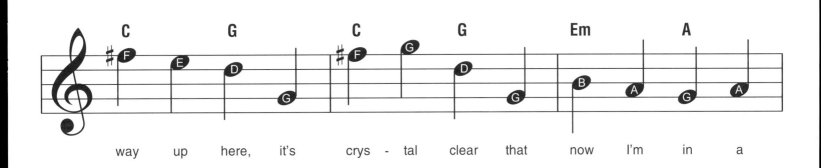

way up here, it's crys - tal clear that now I'm in a

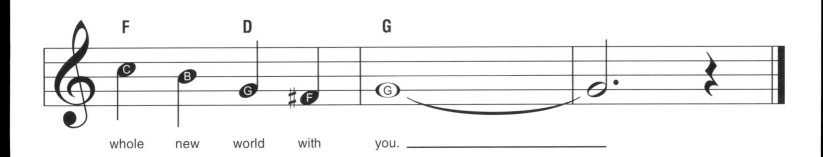

whole new world with you. _____

Winnie the Pooh
from THE MANY ADVENTURES OF WINNIE THE POOH

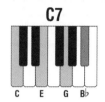
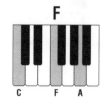
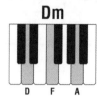

Words and Music by Richard M. Sherman
and Robert B. Sherman

Moderately

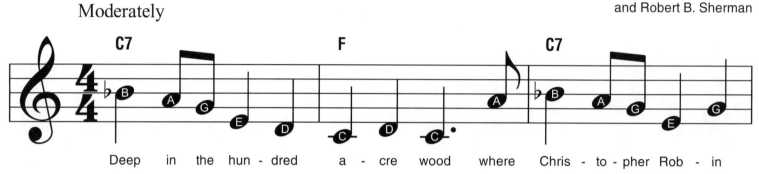

Deep in the hun - dred a - cre wood where Chris - to - pher Rob - in

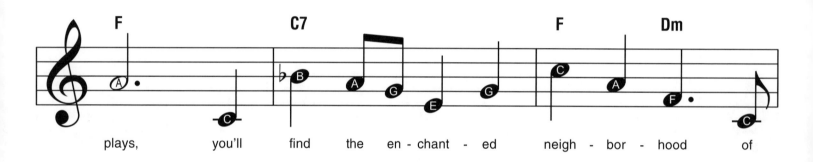

plays, you'll find the en - chant - ed neigh - bor - hood of

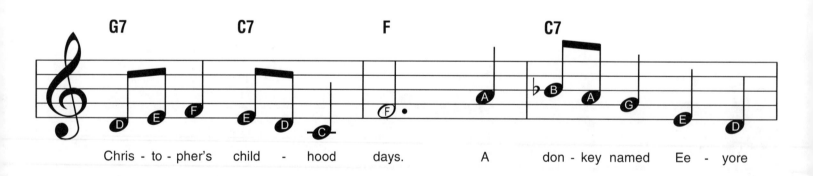

Chris - to - pher's child - hood days. A don - key named Ee - yore

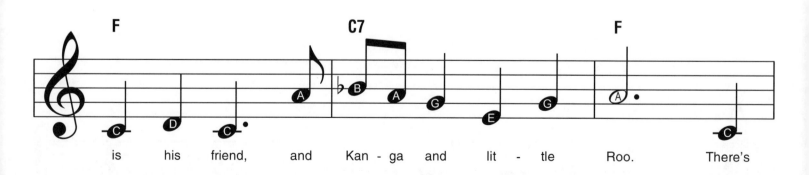

is his friend, and Kan - ga and lit - tle Roo. There's

© 1963 Wonderland Music Company, Inc.
Copyright Renewed.
All Rights Reserved. Used by Permission.

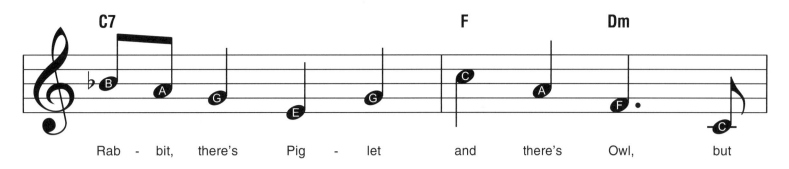

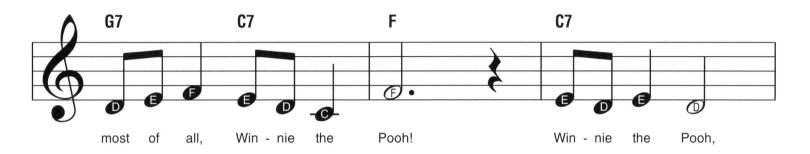

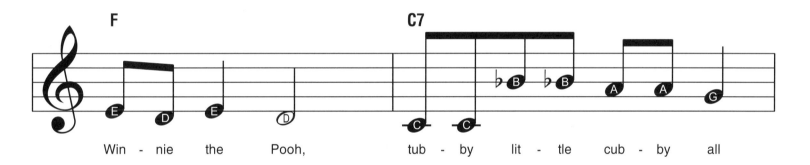

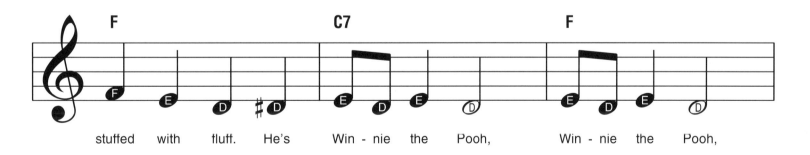

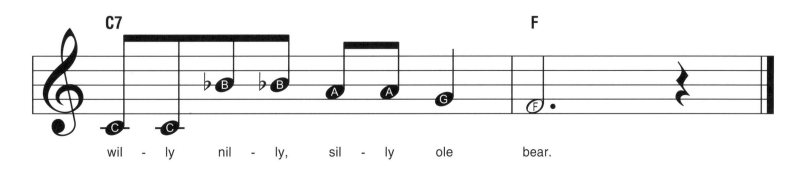

With a Smile and a Song
from SNOW WHITE AND THE SEVEN DWARFS

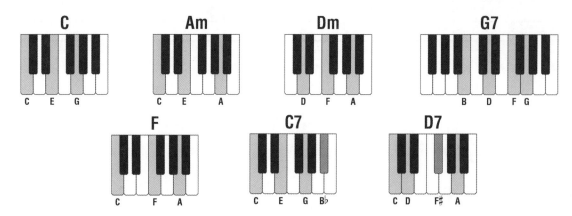

Words by Larry Morey
Music by Frank Churchill

Moderately

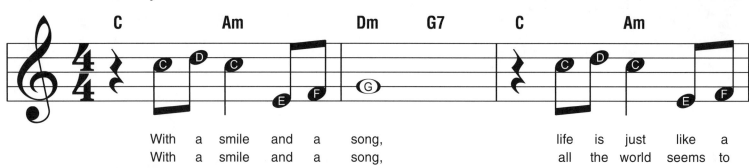

With a smile and a song,   life is just like a
With a smile and a song,   all the world seems to

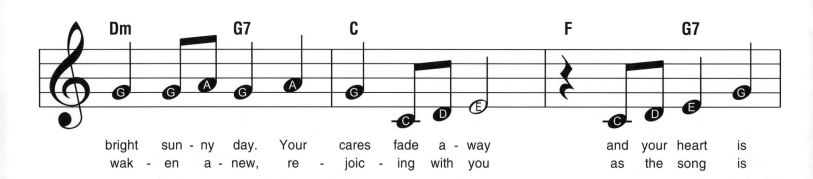

bright sun - ny day. Your cares fade a - way   and your heart is
wak - en a - new, re - joic - ing with you   as the song is

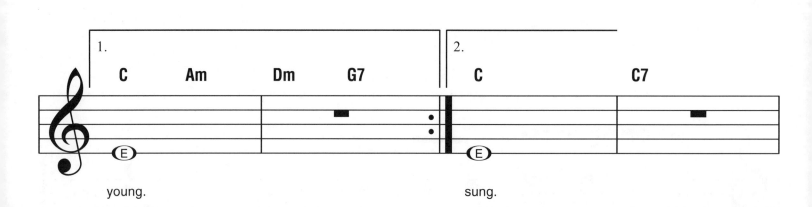

1. young.

2. sung.

Copyright © 1937 by Bourne Co. (ASCAP)
Copyright Renewed.
International Copyright Secured.   All Rights Reserved.

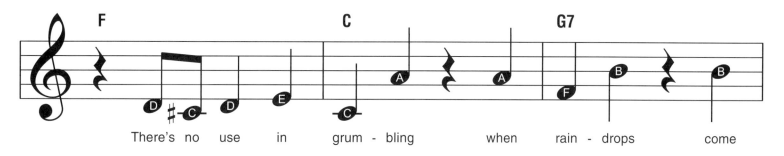

There's no use in grum - bling when rain - drops come

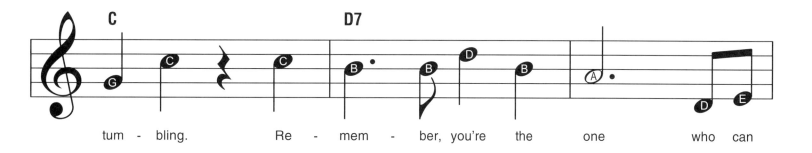

tum - bling. Re - mem - ber, you're the one who can

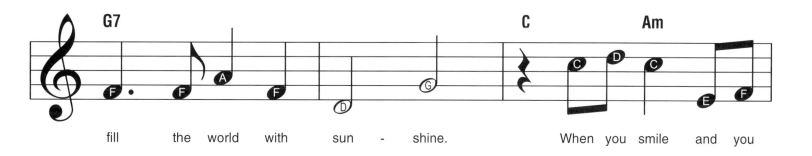

fill the world with sun - shine. When you smile and you

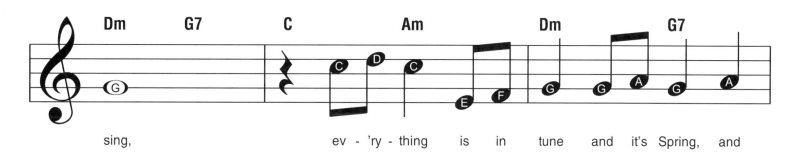

sing, ev - 'ry - thing is in tune and it's Spring, and

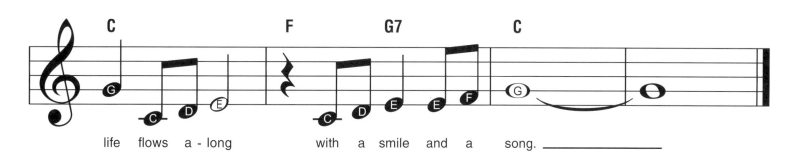

life flows a - long with a smile and a song. _____

The Wonderful Thing About Tiggers

from THE MANY ADVENTURES OF WINNIE THE POOH

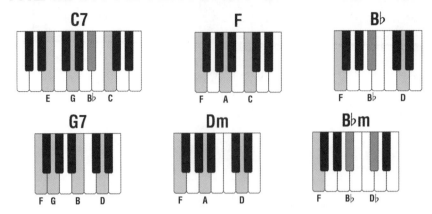

Words and Music by Richard M. Sherman
and Robert B. Sherman

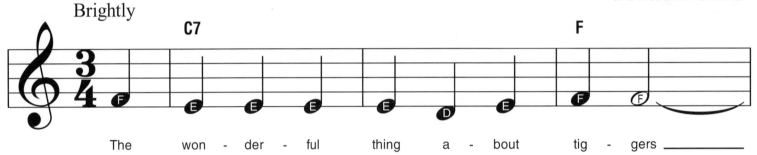

The won - der - ful thing a - bout tig - gers _____

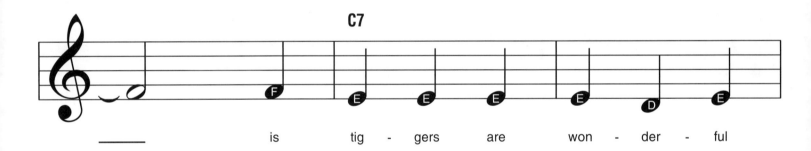

_____ is tig - gers are won - der - ful

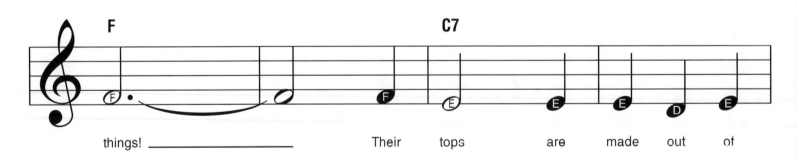

things! _____ Their tops are made out of

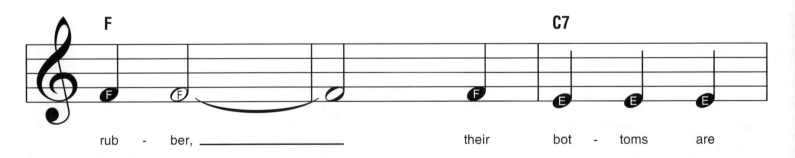

rub - ber, _____ their bot - toms are

© 1964 Wonderland Music Company, Inc.
Copyright Renewed.
All Rights Reserved. Used by Permission.

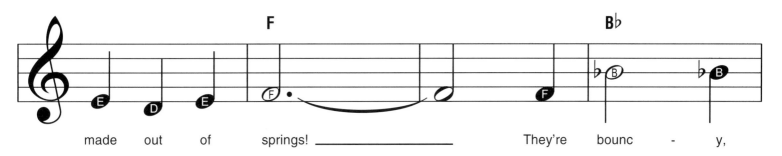

made out of springs! _____ They're bounc - y,

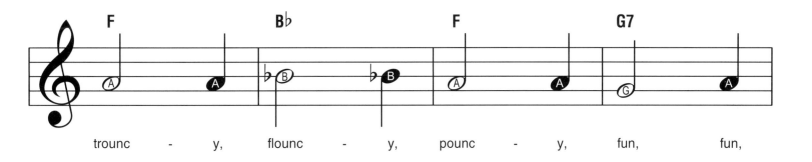

trounc - y, flounc - y, pounc - y, fun, fun,

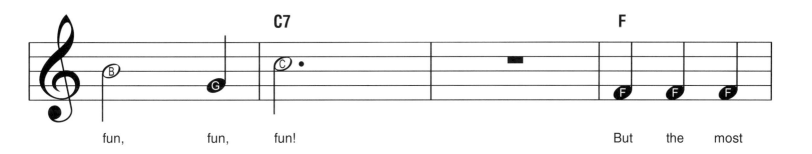

fun, fun, fun! But the most

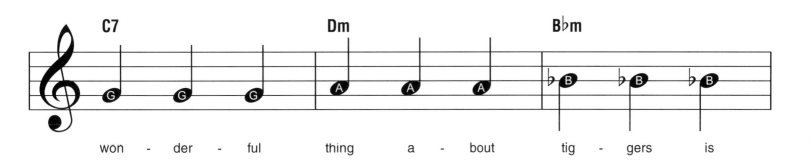

won - der - ful thing a - bout tig - gers is

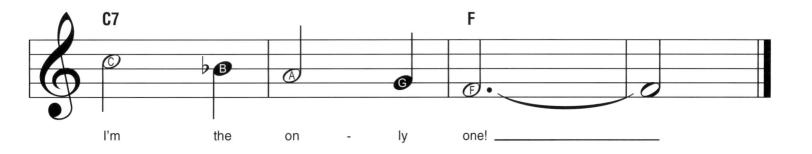

I'm the on - ly one! _____

Wringle Wrangle
from WESTWARD HO, THE WAGONS!

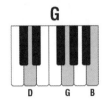
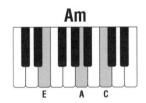
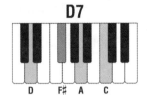

Words and Music by
Stan Jones

Lively
(no chord)

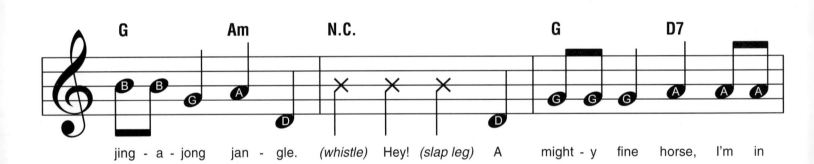

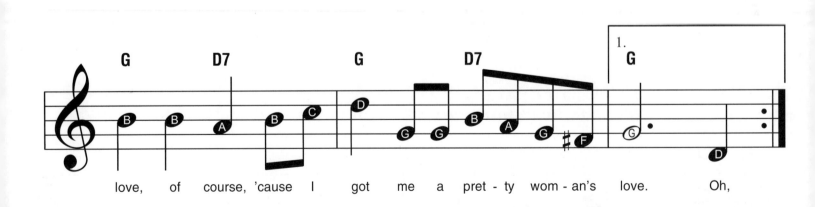

© 1956 Walt Disney Music Company
Copyright Renewed.
All Rights Reserved. Used by Permission.

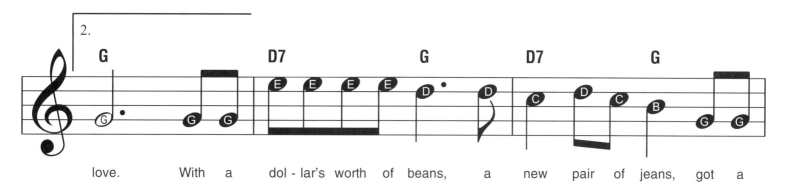

love. With a dol-lar's worth of beans, a new pair of jeans, got a

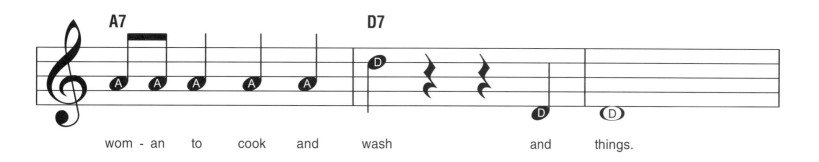

wom - an to cook and wash and things.

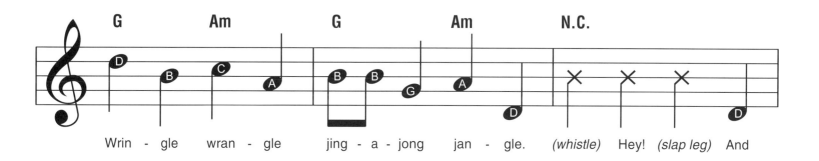

Wrin - gle wran - gle jing - a - jong jan - gle. *(whistle)* Hey! *(slap leg)* And

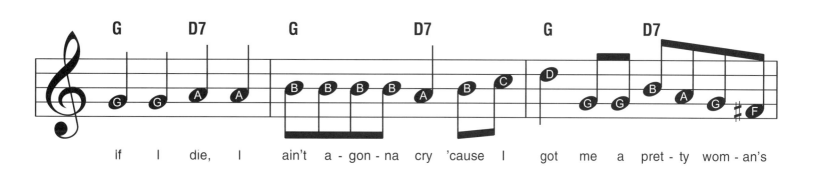

If I die, I ain't a - gon - na cry 'cause I got me a pret - ty wom - an's

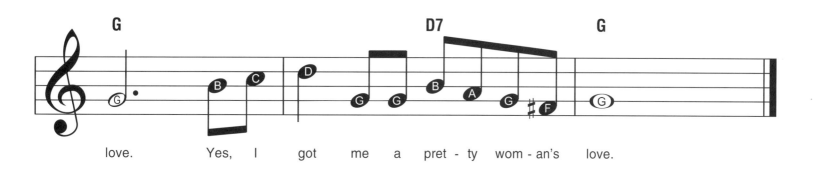

love. Yes, I got me a pret - ty wom - an's love.

Yo Ho
(A Pirate's Life for Me)
from PIRATES OF THE CARIBBEAN
at Disneyland Resort® and Magic Kingdom® Park

Words by Xavier Atencio
Music by George Bruns

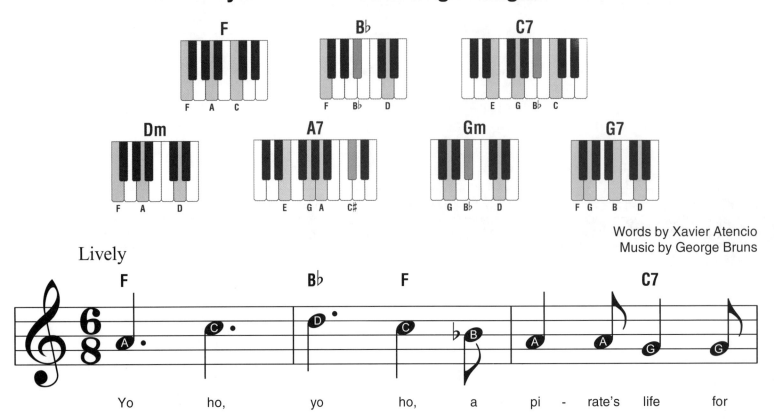

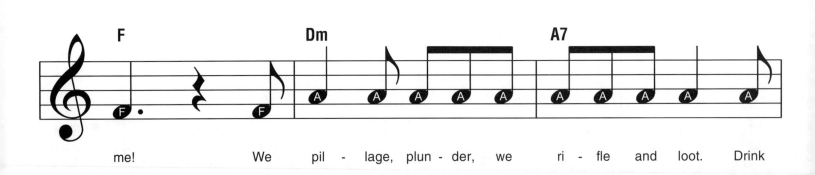

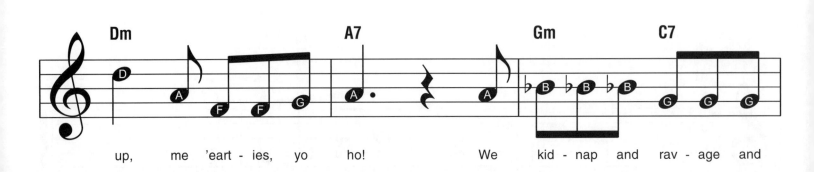

© 1967 Walt Disney Music Company
Copyright Renewed.
All Rights Reserved. Used by Permission.

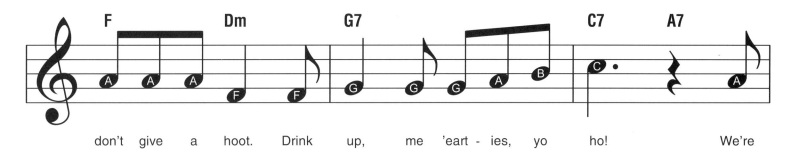

don't give a hoot. Drink up, me 'eart - ies, yo ho! We're

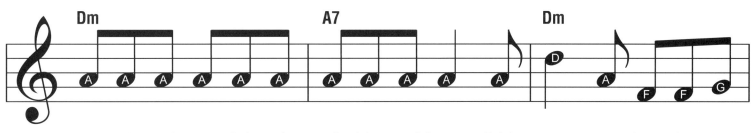

ras - cals and scoun-drels, we're vil - lains and knaves. Drink up, me 'eart - ies, yo

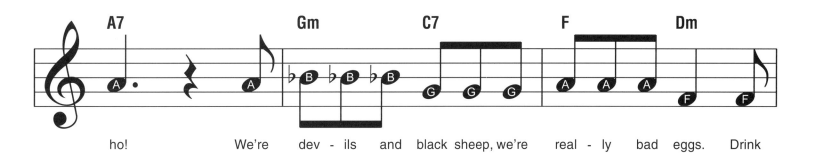

ho! We're dev - ils and black sheep, we're real - ly bad eggs. Drink

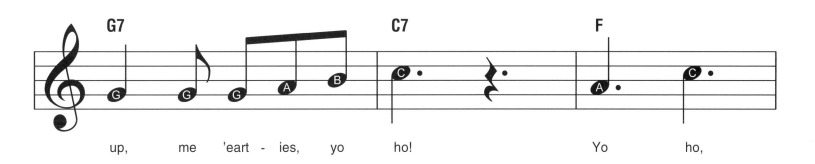

up, me 'eart - ies, yo ho! Yo ho,

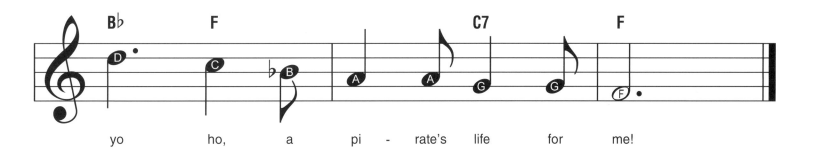

yo ho, a pi - rate's life for me!

You Can Fly! You Can Fly! You Can Fly!

from PETER PAN

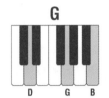 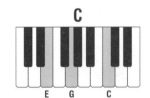 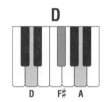 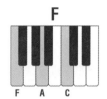 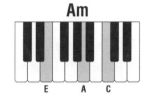

Words by Sammy Cahn
Music by Sammy Fain

Moderately fast

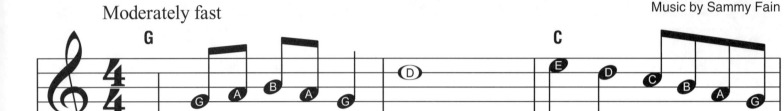

Think   of   the   pres - ents   you're   brought,   an - y   mer - ry   lit - tle
When   there's   a   smile   in   your   heart,   there's   no   bet - ter   time   to

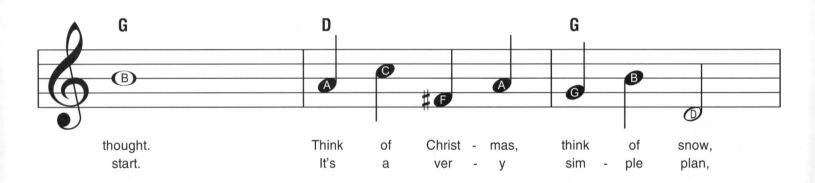

thought.   Think   of   Christ - mas,   think   of   snow,
start.   It's   a   ver - y   sim - ple   plan,

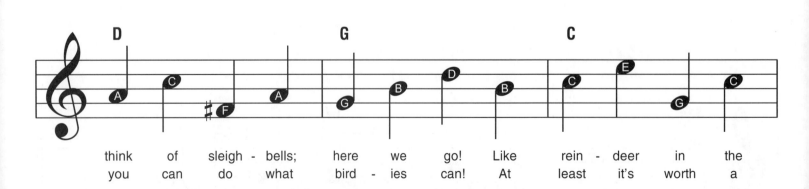

think   of   sleigh - bells;   here   we   go!   Like   rein - deer   in   the
you   can   do   what   bird - ies   can!   At   least   it's   worth   a

© 1951 Walt Disney Music Company
Copyright Renewed.
All Rights Reserved. Used by Permission.

111

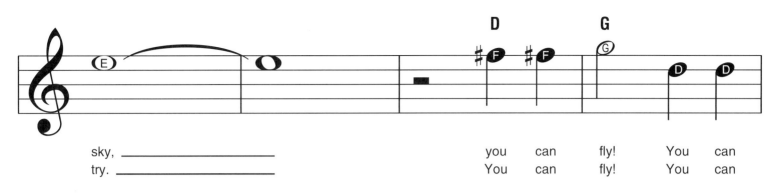

sky, _____ you can fly! You can
try. _____ You can fly! You can

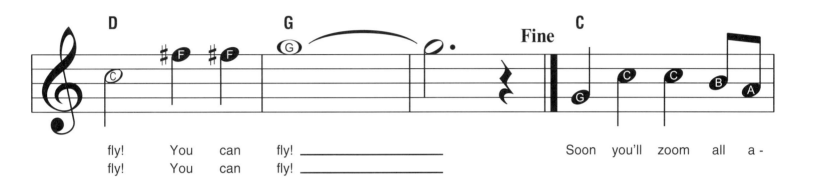

fly! You can fly! _____ Soon you'll zoom all a-
fly! You can fly! _____

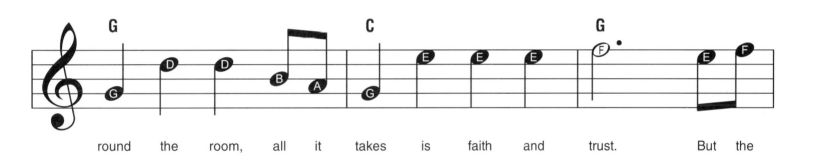

round the room, all it takes is faith and trust. But the

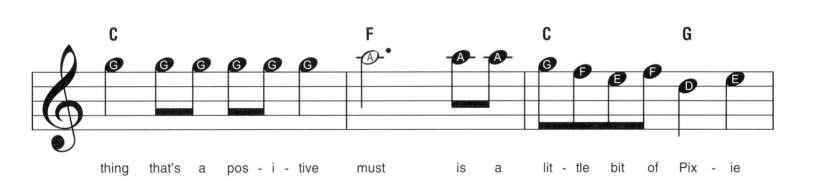

thing that's a pos - i - tive must is a lit - tle bit of Pix - ie

D.C. al Fine
(Return to beginning and play to Fine)

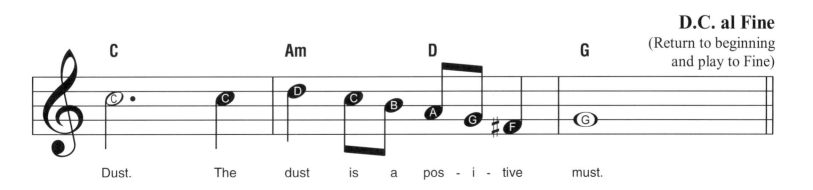

Dust. The dust is a pos - i - tive must.

You'll Be in My Heart
(Pop Version)
from TARZAN™

Words and Music by
Phil Collins

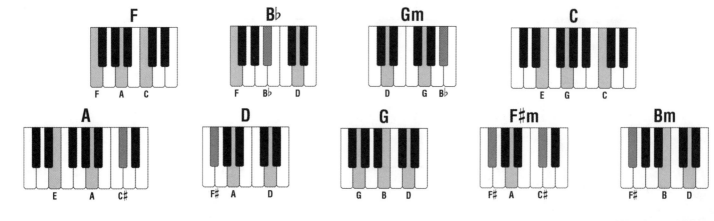

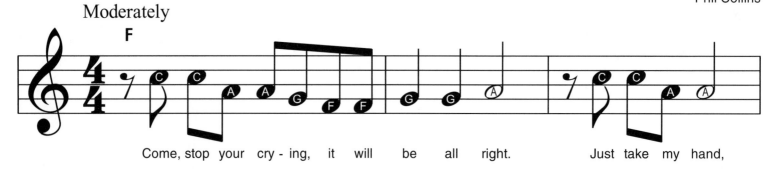

Come, stop your cry-ing, it will be all right. Just take my hand,

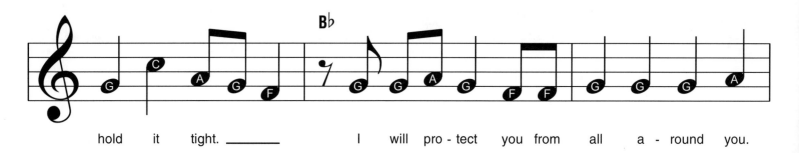

hold it tight. _____ I will pro-tect you from all a-round you.

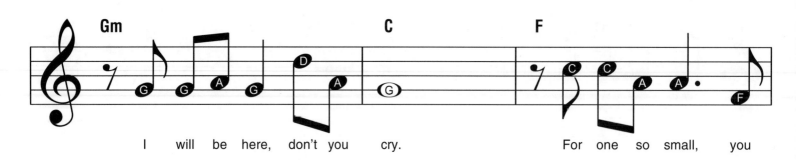

I will be here, don't you cry. For one so small, you

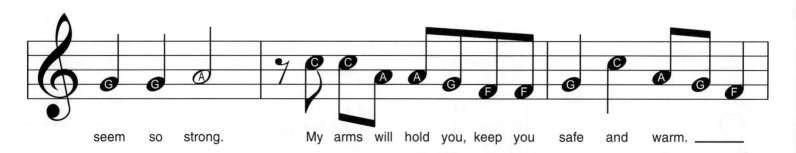

seem so strong. My arms will hold you, keep you safe and warm. _____

© 1999 Edgar Rice Burroughs, Inc. and Walt Disney Music Company
All Rights Reserved. Used by Permission.

Zip-A-Dee-Doo-Dah
from SONG OF THE SOUTH

Words by Ray Gilbert
Music by Allie Wrubel

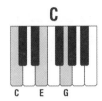
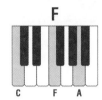
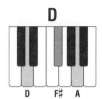

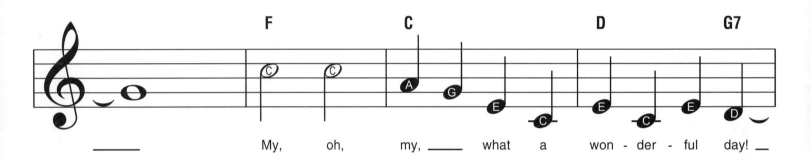

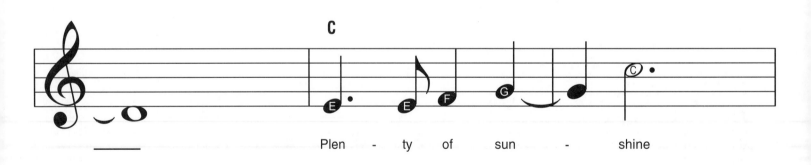

© 1945 Walt Disney Music Company
Copyright Renewed.
All Rights Reserved. Used by Permission.

You've Got a Friend in Me
from TOY STORY

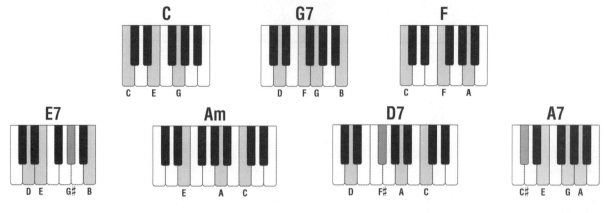

Music and Lyrics by
Randy Newman

Moderate Shuffle

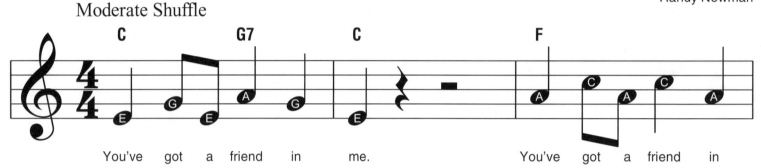

You've got a friend in me. You've got a friend in

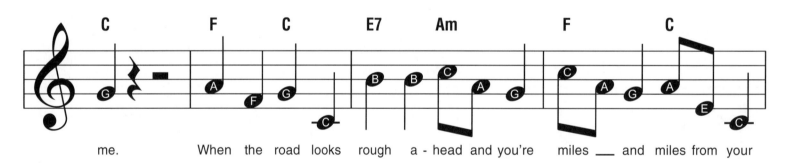

me. When the road looks rough a-head and you're miles ___ and miles from your

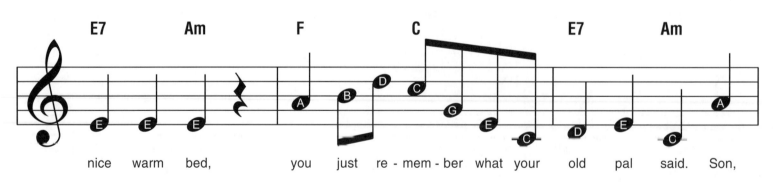

nice warm bed, you just re-mem-ber what your old pal said. Son,

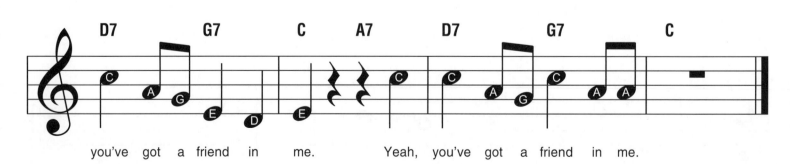

you've got a friend in me. Yeah, you've got a friend in me.

© 1995 Walt Disney Music Company
All Rights Reserved. Used by Permission.

SUPER EASY SONGBOOK

It's super easy! This series features accessible arrangements for piano, with simple right-hand melody, letter names inside each note, and basic left-hand chord diagrams. Perfect for players of all ages!

THE BEATLES
00198161.. $14.99

BROADWAY
00193871.. $14.99

JOHNNY CASH
00287524 .... $9.99

CHRISTMAS CAROLS
00277955 .... $14.99

CHRISTMAS SONGS
00236850 .... $14.99

CLASSICAL
00194693.. $14.99

COUNTRY
00285257 .... $14.99

DISNEY
00199558.. $14.99

FOUR CHORD SONGS
00249533 .... $14.99

GOSPEL
00285256... $14.99

HIT SONGS
00194367... $14.99

HYMNS
A00194659 .... $14.99

JAZZ STANDARDS
00233687... $14.99

ELTON JOHN
00298762 .... $9.99

KIDS' SONGS
00198009... $14.99

THE LION KING
00303511 .... $9.99

ANDREW LLOYD WEBBER
00249580 .... $14.99

MOVIE SONGS
00233670 .... $14.99

POP STANDARDS
00233770... $14.99

QUEEN
00294889... $9.99

ED SHEERAN
00287525... $9.99

THREE CHORD SONGS
00249664 .... $14.99

TOP HITS
00300405 .... $9.99

HAL•LEONARD®
WWW.HALLEONARD.COM

Prices, contents and availability subject to change without notice.

Disney Characters and Artwork TM & © 2019 Disney

HAL LEONARD PRESENTS
FAKE BOOKS FOR BEGINNERS!

Entry-level fake books! These books feature larger-than-most fake book notation with simplified harmonies and melodies – and all songs are in the key of C. An introduction addresses basic instruction on playing from a fake book.

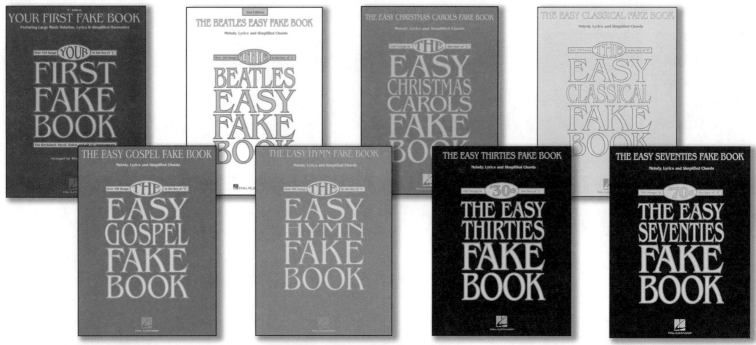

YOUR FIRST FAKE BOOK
00240112............$20.50

THE EASY FAKE BOOK
00240144............$19.99

THE SIMPLIFIED FAKE BOOK
00240168............$19.95

THE BEATLES EASY FAKE BOOK – 2ND EDITION
00171200............$25.00

THE EASY BROADWAY FAKE BOOK – 2ND EDITION
00276670............$19.99

THE EASY CHILDREN'S FAKE BOOK
00240428............$19.99

THE EASY CHRISTIAN FAKE BOOK
00240328............$19.99

THE EASY CHRISTMAS CAROLS FAKE BOOK
00238187............$19.99

THE EASY CHRISTMAS SONGS FAKE BOOK
00277913............$19.99

THE EASY CLASSIC ROCK FAKE BOOK
00240389............$24.99

THE EASY CLASSICAL FAKE BOOK
00240262............$19.99

THE EASY COUNTRY FAKE BOOK
00240319............$19.99

THE EASY DISNEY FAKE BOOK – 2ND EDITION
00275405............$19.99

THE EASY FOLKSONG FAKE BOOK
00240360............$19.99

THE EASY 4-CHORD FAKE BOOK
00118752............$19.99

THE EASY G MAJOR FAKE BOOK
00142279............$19.99

THE EASY GOSPEL FAKE BOOK
00240169............$19.99

THE EASY HYMN FAKE BOOK
00240207............$19.99

THE EASY JAZZ STANDARDS FAKE BOOK
00102346............$19.99

THE EASY LATIN FAKE BOOK
00240333............$19.99

THE EASY LOVE SONGS FAKE BOOK
00159775............$19.99

THE EASY MOVIE FAKE BOOK
00240295............$19.95

THE EASY POP/ROCK FAKE BOOK
00141667............$19.99

THE EASY 3-CHORD FAKE BOOK
00240388............$19.99

THE EASY WORSHIP FAKE BOOK
00240265............$19.99

MORE OF THE EASY WORSHIP FAKE BOOK
00240362............$19.99

THE EASY TWENTIES FAKE BOOK
00240336............$19.99

THE EASY THIRTIES FAKE BOOK
00240335............$19.99

THE EASY FORTIES FAKE BOOK
00240252............$19.99

THE EASY FIFTIES FAKE BOOK
00240255............$19.95

THE EASY SIXTIES FAKE BOOK
00240253............$19.99

THE EASY SEVENTIES FAKE BOOK
00240256............$19.99

THE EASY EIGHTIES FAKE BOOK
00240340............$19.99

THE EASY NINETIES FAKE BOOK
00240341............$19.99

HAL•LEONARD®
www.halleonard.com

Prices, contents and availability subject to change without notice.

0219
128

FOR ORGANS, PIANOS & ELECTRONIC KEYBOARDS

E-Z PLAY® TODAY PUBLICATIONS

The E-Z Play® Today songbook series is the shortest distance between beginning music and playing fun! Check out this list of highlights and visit www.halleonard.com for a complete listing of all volumes and songlists.

HAL•LEONARD®

Prices, contents, and availability subject to change without notice.